UNSUNG HEROES

I0263500

WRITTEN BY ELEANOR NUNIS
EDITED BY JEANNE TYSSEN
www.dmbooks.org

Disclaimer:

My sister Jeanne and I were too young to remember the events of war but over the years, we have listened to our mother and grandparents' stories. Dad would not talk about the war but one day, quite by chance he let his guard down and gave me a glimpse of what he went through.

I've tried to be true to my parents' memories but given the passage of time, I no longer have them around to verify details and the accuracy of events and places. I have obtained some historical information from various sources and included them where relevant.

The war claimed the lives of so many loved ones and friends. Any distress caused in reading this account was never my intent.

Eleanor

Published in 2017 by DMBOOKS (Singapore) to mark the 75th anniversary of World War II in Asia.

For more information or media enquiries, please log on to www.dmbooks.org or email the author at eleanornunis@gmail.com

ISBN (Ebook): 978-981-11-2918-6
ISBN (Paperback): 978-981-11-2917-9
First edition (Ebook) – June 15 2017
First edition (Paperback) – September 1 2017

Copyright © Eleanor Nunis, 2017

All rights reserved. No part of this publication may be reproduced, stored in a retrieval system, or transmitted, in any form or by any means without the prior written permission of the author, nor be otherwise circulated in any form of binding or cover other than that in which it is published and without a similar condition being imposed on the subsequent purchaser.

Cover photography: David Tyssen

Printed by CreateSpace

Dedicated to

Ralph and Edna, Ivy and Justin, Jack and Bill

Their faith, love, sacrifice and endurance has formed the bedrock of my life and for this, I thank them.

INTRODUCTION

In 1941 while the conflict in Europe raged on, there were rumours of a Japanese threat to Malaya and Singapore. The Japanese Empire was already at war with the Republic of China and now it appeared that Singapore was also in its sights.

Singapore, a strategically important stronghold in the Asia-Pacific region for Britain, would give Japan an extremely valuable advantage if captured. Malaya too would be a great economic asset with its resources, especially rubber and tin. Significantly, it would also destabilise Britain's hold on the Far East.

Initially, there was little concern about the Japanese threat to Malaya and Singapore in the British High Command and even if there was, the majority of resources were deployed in Europe to defend Britain itself.

The island of Singapore, situated at the southernmost tip of the Malay Peninsula, was well fortified and was considered impregnable.

Malaya was not seriously considered as a target as it was covered by thick impenetrable jungle which was generally thought to be too difficult for an army to traverse.

CHAPTER 1
THE STANLEYS

Prior to World War II, the Stanley family lived in Muar, a quiet laid-back town, situated at the mouth of the Muar River on the south-western coast of Malaya. It was picturesque, especially at night, when the moon rose over the banks of the river, shedding its golden glow through the trees at the cape or 'Tanjung' as it is called in Malay and peeping over the dome of the grand white Mosque nearby.

Forty-seven kilometres to the north of Muar is the famous city of Malacca. Its strategic position on the coast of Malaya in the Straits of Malacca had made it an important port for maritime trade in the Asian region.

It would become a bustling centre for the spice trade, as the Malacca Straits shortened the trade route between India and China. Sea-faring European traders realised its importance and from early 16th century to the middle of the 20th century, Malacca would be under the control of three different European colonial powers – the Portuguese, Dutch and British.

Ivy grew up with her two brothers, Norman (fondly nicknamed Jack), and a younger brother William (who was known to everyone as Bill). Their parents were Ralph and Edna Stanley. Ralph was English. His father, Frederick, had trained with the Army at Woolwich in London, where he married a local girl, Elizabeth Harding. In the meantime, the island of Singapore was developing into an important trading hub for the East India Company as the spice trade was expanding. When the opportunity arose for someone with suitable qualifications to take up the position of Chief Prison Warden in Singapore, Frederick was immediately interested.

At first, Elizabeth, his wife, was not too sure that it was a good idea especially for little Frank, their young son. However, it did not take Frederick long to convince her. He pointed out that not only would they be going to a beautiful tropical island, financially they would be much better off. It was not long before he, his wife and son Frank were on the ship making the voyage to the Far East. Ralph and his sister, Ethel were born in Singapore, Ralph in 1892, Ethel, a couple of years later.

Adapting to the relentless hot and tropical weather was a challenge, particularly for Elizabeth, but having servants to do the housework made life a lot easier. The children on the other hand, especially Ralph and his sister, Ethel, had no problems at all. The children enjoyed growing up in Singapore. They spent a lot of time outdoors and frequently went bike riding and swimming with their friends. It was a happy, carefree childhood. The youngest son, Arthur, was born in England after the whole family returned to their home country in the early nineteen-hundreds.

Ralph had developed a love for Singapore and also Malaya, where he had spent many family holidays. After completing his education, Ralph worked for a while in England, before deciding he would like to return to the place of his birth. He left England in 1914 and took up the position of manager of a rubber plantation in the Malayan state of Johore. He was a tall and handsome twenty-three-year-old. With tattoos on arms and chest, this imposing man cut an impressive figure in the town.

Ralph was playing the role of Santa Claus at a Christmas party in Singapore when he met Edna, an attractive seventeen-year-old. Edna was stylish and graceful, with her glossy black hair placed high up on her head in a bun. Ralph was immediately attracted to her and lost no time in striking up a friendship with the beautiful young lady. It was not long before he approached her father, Thomas Miles, for permission to court her and after a year, he officially wrote to him to ask for her hand in marriage. Edna and Ralph married on 25th of November 1916 at the Catholic Cathedral of the Good Shepherd in Singapore.

Edna was a Eurasian, having both European and Asian heritage. The spice trade had attracted many Europeans to Asia and subsequently there were many intermarriages with members of the local Asian communities. Children from these mixed race marriages were known as 'Eurasian'. The majority of Malayan

Eurasians can trace their European ancestry to the Portuguese, Dutch or British, while their Asian lineage had roots in the Chinese, Malay or Indian communities.

Edna's family had a long association with Malaya, in fact, her grandfather, Captain Robert Miles had famously gone down with his ship, the *S.S Benton* (aka *S.S. Bentan*), in the Malacca Straits following a calamitous accident between his ship and the *S.S Fair Penang*. The captain of the *Fair Penang* was charged with culpable homicide following the incident as 150 people had perished. The case generated much publicity throughout the shipping world at the time.

Cooking was one of Edna's talents. She excelled at catering cakes and *makan kechil*, Eastern style hors d'oeuvre for parties or private functions. Friends and neighbours frequently approached Edna to cater for their parties. She was also well known for her skill at creating a variety of paper flowers. Ralph, in the meantime, took up further studies in Public Health and became a Health Inspector, stationed in Singapore but working in both Singapore and Johore Bahru, on the southern tip of Malaya.

In the next few years, Edna would present him with a beautiful daughter, Ivy, followed by two bouncing baby boys, Jack and Bill. Ralph, a dedicated father and loving husband, was also passionate about his work. From time to time there were outbreaks of disease in the impoverished and overcrowded areas of Singapore and Ralph volunteered for the unenviable task of supervising the burning of huts to prevent the disease from spreading. He was held in high regard for his work.

At the beginning of the twentieth century, commodities like rubber, tin and palm oil from Malaya were being transported by ferry across the Johore Straits to Singapore. The volume of traffic and the demand for ferries rose rapidly, causing increasing congestion. As Singapore was a British colony, the British government decided to build a causeway to link the Peninsula of Malaya to the island. It was an ambitious plan that would provide a road and rail link, as well as piped water into Singapore. The Johore-Singapore Causeway was officially opened in June 1924. Along with the many dignitaries, Ralph was invited to be one of the first to cross the newly-built Causeway on his motor-bike.

Shortly after, Ralph was appointed Chief Health Inspector of Muar, in the state of Johore. Edna was delighted, for with it came a spacious two-storey home in Muar, ideal for raising a young family. Besides his work in Health, Ralph played a major role in designing the beautiful botanic gardens at the 'Tanjung' which is now known as Tanjong Emas.

CHAPTER 2
IVY

As a child, Ivy was a 'tom-boy', with a cheeky sense of fun and adventure. She was fearless and did whatever her brothers would do. They inherited their father's mischievous nature and were always up for challenging adventures. There was always a sparkle in their eyes as they got up to pranks or teased one another.

In school, Ivy loved to tease her classmates as well. She would play a joke on them, then run away, climb up a tree, sit on a branch, her legs dangling over and call out, "You can't catch me." Some of the boys in her class would jump up and try to pull her down by her legs. One day, they succeeded and Ivy fell down with a heavy thump on her bottom and a nasty gash in her right thigh. It was now the boys' turn to taunt her, as she winced with pain.

The wound became infected and consequently when she was about seven years old, Ivy developed a bone disease of the right hip and leg. Her days were spent in the hospital, undergoing one operation after another. She went through excruciating pain as bits of infected bone kept breaking off and pierced through her wounds. This problem would plague her intermittently for years. During these times, her parents had difficulty watching her struggle to be brave.

However, as soon as she was well enough to be home again, she joined her brothers and cousins in their escapades as much as she could, playing hide and seek, or chasing one another around the house or in the garden. As time went by, some of her male cousins had motorbikes and she had great pleasure climbing on the back seat and going for a joyride. Family and friends were always welcomed to the house and there were parties with lots of laughter. Ivy took part in the activities requiring the minimum physical effort of her lower limbs but the infection in her hip and leg would flare up time and again, and her fun-loving days were getting fewer and fewer. She accepted the restrictions placed on her because of her disability, but when she was in her early teens she started to yearn to be on the dance floor like her cousins. Deep and ugly scars and the shortening of her right leg were evidence of several operations she had undergone and Ivy developed a marked limp. As Ivy became more conscious of her awkward gait, she gradually withdrew into herself.

One day, while Ivy was at home, she overheard a conversation between her mother and her Aunt Muriel. In a soft voice, Edna was telling her sister that the specialist had spoken to Ralph and herself the day before. He warned them that Ivy's future was uncertain and that they should prepare themselves for the worst. Muriel, confused and distressed, asked what he meant by that. Edna, in a teary voice, said he explained that over the years, the recurring infection and operations, had taken its toll on the bone density and structure of Ivy's hip. There was a likelihood that one day when Ivy placed her weight on the affected leg, the hip joint could give way and the surgical team may not be able to save her.

Ivy heard her mother sobbing. She did not let her mother know what she had overheard as she did not wish to put her through more distress. Instead, she confided in Eileen and Enid, two of her cousins that she was closest to. They were horrified that after all the suffering she had gone through, worse may come. "We're so sorry," they sobbed. "It's so unfair."

"I don't know what to do," Ivy whispered, trying not to cry.

There was a silence and finally one of them said, "I wouldn't have the courage to keep on going," and the other nodded in agreement.

Over the next few weeks, Ivy went through bouts of depression and despair. Her mind kept turning over what her cousins had said and she decided they were right. She asked herself, What's the use of living when there is no future ahead? This thought had never crossed her mind before. She refused to eat and she refused to study. Her schooling was already interrupted by her frequent hospital admissions and her family was concerned about her education. They were even more worried about her dark moods. But Ivy was also a fighter. She did a lot of soul-searching through this difficult time and finally decided that however short her life might be, she was going to live it to the full.

Ivy started to make plans. She would no longer worry about being cautious with every step she took. Instead, she was going to learn to dance. She knew her parents would not agree to it, so she enlisted her cousins' help.

Her determination and coaxing finally paid off; she locked her bedroom door and the dancing lessons commenced. When her parents realised what was happening, they tried to stop her but could not get in without breaking down the door. No amount of scolding or pleading had any effect. Reluctantly they realised that they had to accept that she was old enough to decide how she would live her life. Dancing would be one of her greatest joys, an activity she could participate in whenever she was out of the hospital.

CHAPTER 3
THE MONTEIROS

It was around this time, in 1933, when Justin Monteiro, an aspiring young teacher, came to Muar. His brother, Swithin, the eldest son of fifteen children in the family, had found him a position at St. Andrew's Private school under Fr. Renee Ashnes, the local Parish priest. Unlike the Government schools, which had separate Primary and Secondary schools, children who enrolled at this Private Primary school continued their education till they completed their Secondary level. Justin was proficient at teaching at both Primary and Secondary school levels.

His father, Fabian, a Eurasian of Portuguese/Spanish descent, had retired from Civil

Service in Kuala Lumpur and settled in Muar with his wife, Josephine in the early 1930's. Justin, his sisters, Henrietta and Patricia and his brother, Oswald (Osie) all lived with their parents. Osie was the only one still attending school. He became friends with Jack and Bill Stanley and their cousins who were at the same Secondary School.

Swithin lived in Kluang, a town not far from Muar, with his wife, Eileen and daughter, Tessie. He was Headmaster at a Secondary School. Another brother, Royston (Roy) was a teacher in Muar at the Government English Primary School (GEPS). Nearly all of Justin's older siblings chose to remain in Kuala Lumpur or Seremban. Many were married and had children.

Justin, at 21 years of age, although considered good-looking was quiet and shy and spent most of his time playing and composing music with Roy. The brothers were talented musicians. They composed a song, 'The Muarian Moon' with Justin writing the music and Roy, the words. The headmistress of GEPS, Mrs Milne, was impressed with the song and offered to help the brothers take it a step further. Besides undertaking the arrangement, she also had the song translated and sung in

Malay by another teacher at the school. 'His Master's Voice' produced the record in 1935.

MUARIAN MOON

Muar's long warm day is slowly dying,
Brightness is leaving Heaven's face
Birds to their nests are swiftly flying
And the sun seeks his resting place.
Then slowly comes the Queen of Night
Oér dark and dreamy Muar
To shed her light.

Chorus

The pale silent Mosque will be lit very soon
For low in the sky rides the Muarian Moon
The treetops are blowing, the calm rivers flowing
And faint lights are glowing
Over dark waters blue
The lazy Muar River will be lit very soon
For low in the sky rides the Muarian Moon.

Children are done with books and learning

> *Fading light tells them play must cease*
> *In towns and kampongs, men are turning*
> *Turning back home for rest and peace.*
> *The peeping moon now shyly gleams*
> *Above the smoky clouds that veil her beams.*

The song was a hit, and the Monteiro brothers became well-known especially in the state of Johore.

Mrs Milne had planned to work in the Far East for a short time only but liked Malaya so much, she put off returning to England until her retirement. Her contribution in advancing the education of the local children was invaluable.

Ralph Stanley loved music and the Monteiro boys' musical talent ensured they were always welcomed to hold musical evenings at the Stanley home. Knowing Justin was a teacher, Edna suggested to her husband that perhaps he could be of some help to their daughter. Justin was asked if he would tutor Ivy while she was in the hospital. At first, Justin hesitated, not sure whether he would be suitable but with a bit of persuasion, agreed to give it a try. Edna approached the hospital staff and found them willing to cooperate with her plan as they were well acquainted with Ivy's situation. Justin was then taken to the hospital to meet Ivy herself. She was fourteen years old.

Initially, Ivy was shy and too embarrassed to respond to Justin's tutoring.

Her frequent spells in the hospital had created gaps in her learning. School had become a daunting place as she fell further and further behind in her studies. As a result, her self-esteem was steadily being eroded. But Justin was so kind and patient with her, Ivy began to enjoy his visits. He was sensitive to her feelings and was always on the lookout for signs of fatigue or if she was in pain.

Lessons were specially designed to be engaging and stimulating. She was a quick learner and made excellent progress under his guidance. Whenever she was discharged from the hospital, Justin would go to the house to continue her tutoring. It was not very long before she caught up with the lessons her classmates were doing at school. Over the next couple of years, her confidence grew, with Justin by her side. He became her confidante; her soul mate.

CHAPTER 4
YOUNG LOVE

As time went on, Ivy's hospital admissions became less frequent and her wounds slowly healed. She had decided to leave school just a year before completing her studies and began to think of doing something useful in her life. She appreciated how much Justin had helped her and thought that perhaps she could help others too. She shared her desire with her parents but as they did not know what she could do, they just smiled and said she should relax and enjoy being home.

One day, an idea came into her head. The family home was large and there was a spacious area below that was seldom used, now that she and her siblings had grown up. She excitedly announced her plan to Ralph and Edna. She would gather together the neighbourhood children who could not afford to go to school and teach them to read and write. When her parents looked doubtful, she appealed to her mother, reminding her that she herself often helped the disadvantaged.

Ivy urged Edna to support her as she too would like to do something worthwhile. Ivy was referring to her mother helping those in need whenever she could. Edna was well-known and loved by the local children. She held an annual Christmas party for underprivileged children in the neighbourhood and gave each one of them a small gift. For many, it was the highlight of the year. Ralph and Edna felt very proud of their daughter and said, "Go ahead with your plan, darling." With her parents' blessing and assistance, she started her English classes.

Ivy was close to her brothers who had become dashing young men and were well-liked in the town. The older brother, Jack, was cheeky, loved socialising and having a great time at parties, drinking with friends. He was also an incorrigible flirt. Bill was less of an extrovert and was known to be gentle and caring. He was intelligent, wrote poetry and had a secret desire to become a doctor.

The boys were always invited to parties that took place among the Eurasian families in Muar. Jack always kept an eye out for Bill. When his younger brother was present, Jack, the care-free and fun-loving person also took on a protective role.

Bill, easy going and not wanting to offend anyone could be persuaded to drink too much. If a situation arose that he may be getting himself into trouble, Jack would intervene the minute he thought Bill needed his help. Bill, still in his late teens, had not yet learned how to handle alcohol like his brother and cousins.

At the same time, they were also rivals for the attention of the same young lady in their group. She was a newcomer and came from the community of Eurasians in Malacca. Bill seemed to have out-manoeuvred his brother when Millicent (Millie) agreed to go out with him.

Ivy found life exhilarating. She could now participate in most activities where once she was restricted to the role of observer. And she danced! A new heel specifically made and attached to her right shoe, enabled her to move more gracefully across the floor.

It was a time when relationships were blooming. A romance developed between Ivy's cousin, Enid and Justin's brother, Roy. They soon married. Justin's sisters, Henrietta and Patricia also joined the ranks of the newly-weds.

Justin became Ivy's constant companion and joined her in her outings with her brothers and cousins. She wore her hair in ringlets and she was beautiful in Justin's eyes. 'The most beautiful girl in the world', he would say to all his friends.

Their favourite meeting place was the Tanjung, with its tall trees and gardens. All the cousins and friends met there. At sunset, a spectacular display of colour lit up the sky producing a reflection and radiant glow on the river Muar below.

CHAPTER 5
JUSTIN AND IVY

Ivy and Justin had fallen in love. They began to talk of marriage. They were dubbed *Blankasts*, a Malay word for Sting Ray, the type which always travels in pairs. However, when it became apparent that the young couple were in love with each other, Ivy's father entirely disapproved of their relationship. Though Justin was doing well in his teaching career, he still lived with his mother and brother. Ralph firmly believed that financially, Justin would not be able to support Ivy, in the way she was accustomed.

Ralph had nothing against him as a person. In fact, he found Justin very likeable. He was soft-spoken and considerate of others. Ralph's concern was for Ivy's well-being. The years of suffering and numerous operations she had endured made him extremely protective of his 'Princess'. Ralph had ensured she received the best treatment possible, even engaging a carer when she was at home, to provide extra help when needed. Ralph realised it was close to three years since her last hospitalisation and the problems that had dogged her for so long may be gone forever. But what if the leg infection returned? Only time could tell. He was convinced it was too soon for Ivy to get involved in a serious relationship, as she was only twenty.

Justin was no longer welcomed to the Stanley home. This was heart-wrenching for Ivy and Justin and affected their close-knit group. Jack, who loved his sister, was also Ralph's right-hand man. When Ralph disapproved of Justin, Jack upheld his father's wishes and did not encourage Justin's advances to his sister. This led to tension between Ivy and Jack. Ivy tried to reason with him but Jack was resolute and unmoved. Ivy felt her brother was unjust and kept her distance from him. In the meantime, Justin was despondent. He could not talk to Ivy and only occasionally he would see her from a distance. He also missed the camaraderie of his friendship group as they often socialised in Ralph's home.

One night, while the Stanley brothers had their cousins over, Justin tried to join them without Ralph's knowledge. He stealthily climbed up the wall to their bedroom and tried to get the boys' attention by prising open the window. Jack, seeing a hand on the window-sill, thought it was an intruder and promptly slammed the window onto the hand. Justin fell to the ground and into the bushes with a thump. "It's me, Justin", he said in a loud whisper.

"Justin?" they whispered back, incredulously. "Stay there. We'll come and get you."

Jack quietly went outside and rescued Justin from the bushes. He admonished him by telling him not to do it again, as it was too dangerous. And he reminded Justin that his father did not approve of him visiting their home.

Bill, on the other hand, hated seeing anyone unhappy, especially his sister, and before long, carried messages between Justin and Ivy. It was typical of Bill who had a tender heart and only saw the best in everyone.

It was in one of these secret messages when Justin confirmed his proposal to Ivy; he wrote her this poem:

In my solitude I see
Visions of what's in store for me
You, a happy blushing bride
I, the proud groom by your side.
Very happy we'll then be
You'll belong to only me.

Ivy, almost twenty-one, decided she would marry Justin without her father's consent. She approached her mother, saying, "I love Justin and he loves me. He has helped me find confidence in myself again. I know I can't live without him." Ivy implored Edna to speak to her father. To tell him that she loved him very much but she had made up her mind to marry Justin. Arrangements had been made for them to marry at a Church in Kuala Lumpur with a reception to be held at Justin's sister, Belle's home.

With tears in her eyes, Edna listened to Ivy's plea. She understood her husband's love and concern for their daughter's well-being and had not intervened initially. But after hearing Ivy profess her love for Justin and her determination to marry him at all costs, she simply said,

"If you are sure that's what you want, go ahead, my darling."

Ivy packed to go to Kuala Lumpur and was given full support from not only her mother but also her brothers, cousins and friends, who prepared to attend her wedding. Jack, accepting that Ivy and Justin's love for each other could not be thwarted, offered to give his sister away at the wedding ceremony, in place of his father. Just before they drove away from Muar, Jack advised Justin to approach his father and ask for Ivy's hand, saying "You can't leave like this."

Ralph, a man of stature in the town of Muar appeared formidable to Justin, but heeding Jack's advice, he took the courage to go to Ralph in a last attempt for a blessing. This gesture led Ralph to admire Justin's courage and a good relationship developed between them that would last a lifetime. Ralph not only gave his blessing but said regretfully that if it was not so far away, he certainly would attend the wedding. He welcomed Justin into the family and hugged and kissed his beloved daughter.

He also invited them to come live in his home after their marriage. Ivy and Justin were married on the 27th of December 1939.

Ivy's cup of happiness was full. She had a husband who adored her and before long, a beautiful daughter arrived. She was especially precious as Ivy had been told that she could never have children as a result of her diseased hip.

Eleanor (Ellen) was safely delivered by caesarian section, the first of these operations ever performed in Muar.

Ivy and Justin were overjoyed and grateful and so were both their parents and family. Many prayers had been made and the birth was looked upon as an answer to prayer. Their only regret was that Fabian, Justin's father, who was very fond of Ivy, passed away a month before his granddaughter was born. Justin had hoped for a son and would have named him Allan but with the arrival of a girl, the name Eleanor was chosen, as the shortened name, Ellen sounded like Allan.

Justin and Ivy proudly took their daughter to meet their relatives in Seremban and Kuala Lumpur and to thank them for their prayers and good wishes.

In the meantime, around the time Ivy and Justin were celebrating their nuptials, both Roy and Enid had remarried new partners. Roy, who lived in Batu Pahat, a town just south of Muar, married Isabel and Enid married Horace, a lawyer who had his law practice in Muar.

The picturesque Tanjung Emas in Muar (current day) where many young couples would meet. Ralph Stanley played a major role in the design of the gardens at the Tanjung, which overlook the mouth of the Muar River.

The impressive Sultan Ibrahim Mosque adjoining the Tanjung Emas, Muar (current day). At sunset and sunrise, this Muarian landmark could be seen as a striking silhouette against the sky from the Tanjung.

Edna Stanley's parents were Thomas Ramage Miles and Eleanor Phipps. They were married in Singapore c.1885.

Justin's parents, Fabian and Josephine Monteiro c. 1920

A picnic at the Tanjung Emas in Muar, c.1935. Front L to R: Noel and Christine Cornelius (nee Rodrigues), Ivy Stanley, Violet Van Buerle, Ralph Stanley, Holly Van Buerle Back L-R: Edna Stanley and two unknown individuals.

Justin and his brother Roy Monteiro were inspired to compose 'Muarian Moon' from their time spent at the Tanjung in Muar in the mid-1930s. It was produced as a 78rpm gramophone recording by HMV pre-1939.

(Left) The carefree days of Muar in the mid-1930s (L to R) Yvonne and Enid Truitwin, Eileen Campbell and Ivy. (Right): Ivy as a teenager.

Ivy with her cousins c.1935 The Eurasian community in Muar was vibrant and close knit. (L to R): Enid Truitwin, Doris Gaudart, Ivy, Yvonne Truitwin.

Justin and Ivy's Wedding, 27th of December 1939 in Kuala Lumpur.

Justin and Ivy's wedding party outside Belle's home (Justin's sister) in Kuala Lumpur. Many of Justin's family were present but very few of Ivy's family were able to attend. Ivy's father Ralph Stanley was notably absent.

This picture was taken at Ralph and Edna's 25th wedding anniversary at a party in Singapore, just weeks before Bill Stanley's 19th birthday. (L to R): Jack, Edna and Bill Stanley.

*Ralph and Edna's 25th wedding anniversary
on the 25th of November 1941*

*Ivy, Justin, and family at Jeanne's (Jean) Christening in November 1941
a few months before the fall of Singapore.*

CHAPTER 6
INVASION OF MALAYA

The ominous threat of war overshadowed Ivy and Justin's joy.

In 1940, as a precautionary measure, allied troops were sent to Malaya and Singapore and a call was made for local volunteers to join the Defence Forces. The call to fight for the British Empire was heeded, especially by the Eurasians and others who were loyal to the British.

Justin grappled with the call to duty and the agony of leaving his wife and child behind. He shared his dilemma with Ivy, explaining that although he knew Singapore's harbour was well defended and it was unlikely Malaya would be attacked, he felt compelled to answer the call to defend his country. He stressed that by doing so, he would be doing his part to protect his family, should there be a war. Ivy kept silent for a while, a wave of fear sweeping over her. Ivy knew Justin was right. She hated the thought of separation from him but bravely holding back her tears, replied, "I will miss you. You do what you think best, darling."

With his wife's blessing, Justin joined the 4th Battalion of the Straits Settlements Volunteer Force (SSVF), which fell under the command of the British Regular Army. Bill Stanley, Justin's brother-in-law, joined the Royal Army Medical Corps (RAMC) as a medic in 1940. They attended regular training camps but otherwise, life went on as usual.

In late October 1941, Jeanne (Jean) was born. Again, everyone was amazed that Ivy could go to full term. Ivy and Justin were delighted and Ivy, who was becoming an experienced mother, got all the support she needed from her parents, as always. Despite the darkening clouds of war, the children were thriving and Ivy and Justin were happy in their marriage.

On 8th of December 1941, Kota Bahru in the northern state of Kelantan on the Malay Peninsula was invaded by the Japanese. Pearl Harbour, the American naval base in Hawaii was bombed an hour later. It was the start of the Pacific War. Three days later, Penang, an island off the west coast of Malaya was bombed.

While Singapore's guns faced south to defend the island against naval attack, the Japanese enemy, under the command of General Yamashita, had surreptitiously infiltrated Malaya through the thick, dense forests from the north.

Less than two months after Jean was born, Justin and Ivy's worst fear was realised; Justin and Bill were called to serve. They had to leave for Singapore to join their units. Bill would turn nineteen in a couple of months.

The Japanese invasion of Malaya placed the minority group of Eurasians in a precarious position. As Japan was at war with Britain and her allies, the Eurasians were earmarked 'semi-enemy' because of their British or European ancestry and became a specific target along with the Chinese population. Members of the Eurasian community tried various ways to handle the situation, such as to pose as Malay, co-operate with the Japanese or try to escape.

Many groups decided to flee into the Malayan jungle, hoping that they would find refuge there. They believed the thick impenetrable vegetation would make it inaccessible for an army with military equipment.

One of these groups was made up of a number of Ivy's relatives, who included among others, the Hanny, Marshall and Bartlett families. One family member urged Justin to let Ivy and the family come with them. They were leaving for Ulu Tiram, not far from Johore Bahru town, as they felt they would be safe there. As the young couple hesitated, he implored them to make up their minds fast.

Ivy and Justin were tempted. However, Justin was being deployed to a camp in Singapore and he would have no contact with his family if they followed the others to Ulu Tiram. He whispered to Ivy that she should come to Singapore instead. That way they would know if anything happened to either of them. He would make all the arrangements in Singapore and then return to Muar to pick up the family. With Ivy's assent, Justin declined the relative's offer.

Soon the Japanese were advancing steadily southwards, forcing the British and their allies to withdraw and later retreat to Johore. While planes flew overhead, bombing Singapore, the Japanese troops advanced mostly undeterred by the traps and ambushes set up by the allied forces. Some came on foot and many came on bicycles, disguised as the local Malay or Chinese, wearing local farmers' clothing. This confused the defenders and allowed the enemy to move equipment and ammunition swiftly and covertly through the dense jungle. They made their way steadily down the west coast to Muar.

A small squadron of allied aircraft attempted to halt the Japanese advance by bombing the enemy line, but this was to no avail. Despite all efforts, the Japanese pushed through, making their way to the surrounding districts close to the source of the Muar River. Physical encounters ensued and Ivy and family in Muar could hear the bombing and gunfire in the distance. Ralph, who had been waiting for Justin to come as he had promised, now thought seriously about some means of escape.

Edna and Ivy with the children in their arms, would huddle under a table in the family home, hoping to block out some of the terrifying flashes and noise that frightened the children. In a very short space of time, the Japanese made further advances along the Muar River.

In Singapore, Justin was anxiously waiting for permission to take his family out of Malaya. When he heard the news of the impending Japanese advance on Muar, he hastened to request special consideration and was granted leave immediately to go and get them.

There was no transport going north; his only hope was to get a car. Justin approached a taxi driver who refused to drive him despite his plea, and in desperation, Justin drew his gun, held it to the taxi driver's head and ordered him to drive to Muar.

When he got there, he was shocked to see the amount of devastation caused by the bombings. The whole town appeared to be deserted. To his relief, he found Ralph and Edna's home was still intact and the family safe. Ivy was overwhelmingly relieved at seeing Justin again. Justin hurriedly bundled his family into the taxi after arranging for his parents-in-law and his mother, Josephine, to follow them in another taxi, heading south. Justin's sisters, Patricia and Henrietta decided to remain in Muar with their families.

On their arrival in Singapore, Justin settled Ivy and the children, Ralph and Edna, in a boarding house run by a relative, Holly Van Buerle. He then dropped off Josephine at her brother Charles' house, before rejoining his unit.

A few days later, between 14th and 22nd of January 1942, one of the bloodiest battles between the Japanese and the Allies began along the Muar River. It was the last major battle of the Malayan campaign and it was a disaster for the British. The only option left to the Allies was to retreat across the 1.5km Johore Causeway to Singapore and then destroy the Causeway, the only land link from the Malayan mainland to Singapore.

CHAPTER 7
ESCAPE FROM SINGAPORE

On 10th of February, Justin came to the boarding house with urgent news for Ivy. He said the Army would help send her, the children and her mother, out of Singapore, to India or Australia. Unfortunately, Ivy's father could not go as they were only evacuating women and children. On hearing this, Edna was dismayed. She was reluctant to leave Ralph, but he insisted that she go. He reassured his wife that he would be all right, especially if he knew she was safe. Only the thought of Ivy and her grandchildren's safety persuaded Edna to accept the idea of being separated from her husband. Her daughter, given the opportunity of being evacuated to another country with her children, would need help.

Justin emphasised how important it was for Ivy and his mother-in-law to be ready to be picked up the 12th or 13th of February at the latest. He warned that there would be a scramble and to be sure to get on the first ship. He handed Ivy some money to buy what she and the family needed.

That night, the whole family got into a taxi and accompanied Justin to his quarters. This gave them a little more precious time together as a family. As they drove to Justin's camp to drop him off, Ellen, not quite two years old, clung to her Daddy and cried, not wanting to let him go. It was as if she knew that this might be the last time she would see him again.

As the young couple said their heart-wrenching goodbyes, Ivy's world crumbled. She would no longer have her beloved husband for assurance and support. She may never ever see him again. How would she manage, she, caring for two very young children with a crippled hip and leg? Thank goodness her mother was coming with her. It then crossed her mind that she may have to look after Edna too as she was not too strong health-wise and was slowly but progressively losing her hearing. The thought that she had to be brave for her children and mother and the hope that she and Justin would be reunited as a family again someday, helped Ivy pull herself together. "I will guard our daughters with my life," she promised Justin, as the taxi pulled away.

With the future unknown, Ivy and Edna prayed and put their trust in God's care. They packed clothes, food, and filled a box with tinned powdered milk which Ivy had bought with the money Justin left her. All prepared, they waited for their transport. The following day, the army truck carrying other families came to pick them up and they said an emotional goodbye to Ralph and Holly. They knew Ralph was in danger, as he was British and he was being left behind in Singapore. Holly promised that Ralph could continue to stay in the boarding house and they could not thank her enough for all her kindness.

They were driven through the burning city and were dropped off at the harbour which was in complete chaos. People were streaming through, trying to get on the boats to freedom. They first had to report to a desk, where the person-in-charge said, "You cannot take all

these bags with you; just one bag. Leave the rest behind."
Ivy tried to plead but was told it was an order. Ivy had a
basket which she hastily repacked with the barest
necessities. They had to leave everything else behind,
even the box of milk they had bought.

They were hustled into lifeboats and taken out
into the harbour to their steamship, the *Mata Hari*. Ivy,
the young mother, determined not to let panic overwhelm
her, dragged Ellen by the hand and carrying her precious
basket in the other, scrambled onto the ship. Edna
followed, trying to keep her balance as she carried Jean in
her arms. It was the 12th of February, 1942.

The *Mata Hari* was one of around forty-seven
vessels to attempt evacuations from Singapore between
the 12th and 14th of February 1942. It was not heading for
India as many of the passengers believed. The
Commanding Officer, Lieutenant Carston was ordered to
travel by night and to take cover by day on the way to
Batavia, the capital city of the Dutch East Indies. They
were to sail via the Banka Straits.

The ship was grossly overcrowded, with women
and children everywhere, all looking for a place to sleep.
Ivy managed to find a small space below deck for the

family. She put four-month-old Jean to her breast as Edna cuddled Ellen close to her. Both the children were tired and fretful and the wailing of the other children made it even harder to settle them down.

That night, Ivy and Edna quietly said their prayers, and finally, the little ones, lulled by Edna's soft singing of children's hymns and safe in the arms of their mother and Granny, fell asleep. With the girls protected between them, they gave a sigh of relief and closed their eyes. They were on their way to freedom. But their dreams of a safe-haven were short-lived.

CHAPTER 8
CAPTURE

During the two days at sea, the captain of the *Mata Hari* was aware that at least three vessels that left Singapore at the same time as the *Mata Hari* had been attacked and most likely sunk. This included the *Vyner Brooke* and the *Kuala*, both of which were carrying many civilians and Australian nurses escaping Singapore.

In the early morning of 15th of February 1942, chaos erupted. The ship's siren wailed as enemy planes flew above. In the pitch dark, bullets whizzed over the deck. Ominous black silhouettes had appeared beside the ship. Next, blinding searchlights shone onto the *Mata Hari*. Women and children screamed, and Jean went into convulsions. Ivy was terror-stricken. "Get down! Over the children!" Edna urged. Ivy dropped to the floor and she and Edna lay over the children to protect them. There they lay and braced themselves for the worst.

The captain of the *Mata Hari*, Captain Carston, conscious of the fact he was carrying so many women and children, raised the white flag. He was ordered to anchor in Banka Straits until daylight. The Captain informed all on board that he had surrendered the ship. He also instructed them to get ready to vacate the ship, taking only one bag each. Ivy and Edna were devastated and so were the other passengers. Shaken and fearful, the families who had managed somehow to get extra luggage on board, were now frantically shoving things into one bag and throwing out what they could not take.

Ivy went searching for practical items and managed to find a bed sheet for nappies, a towel and two dresses that had been thrown on the deck. She pushed them into her already full basket, then keeping the children close to them, Ivy and Edna awaited their fate.

Their captors boarded at daylight and Ivy, with Jean held tight in her arms, trembled. "Keep calm", Edna whispered as she cradled little Ellen. After a considerable time inspecting the ship and giving instructions to Captain Carston, the Japanese Officers left. When the ship entered Muntok Bay as directed, the petrified prisoners were ordered off the ship and into little boats. They were then rowed to Muntok, a port on Banka Island. Bloodied bodies floated alongside their little boats as they headed to Muntok Pier.

It had been a very long day. Hungry and tired children cried and fretted.

When they arrived on the pier that night, Ivy gently wrapped Ellen and Jean in blankets that had been discarded. She noticed a table on the side of the pier and quickly put the children under the table to protect them from being trampled on. She and Edna also slept under the table.

The next morning, with nothing to eat or drink, all the passengers and crew from the *Mata Hari* along with survivors from the other boats, were made to assemble on the pier. A number of Australian Army nurses joined in the queue. They had managed to get ashore when their ship was sunk. Before commencing on the walk to the Internment Camp, they were first ordered to bow low to their Japanese captors.

Edna carried baby Jean in her arms and Ivy, with her basket on one arm, alternately carried Ellen on her good hip or dragged her along by the hand. It was an interminably long, exhausting journey. The blazing sun beat down on their heads, making their thirst even greater. The dust and dirt from the road caked their faces and cracked their lips. Hunger and lack of sleep also contributed to their distress.

On the way, Edna spied a bottle of water on the side of the road. She picked it up; she did not know whether it was drinkable but being so thirsty, she tasted it. Once she thought it was safe, she let Ivy and the girls have a tiny drink. She then gave a sip to as many internees as possible.

"Only one sip each," she repeated, as she handed the bottle to the grateful recipients.

Hours later, they arrived at a camp in the village of Muntok, a large area with an assortment of buildings including the local cinema. It was here the prisoners were to be held and processed before being sent to the various POW camps in the region. The women entered with apprehension, not knowing what was in store for them. Then they saw a couple of water taps in the grounds.

"Water! Water!" they cried and ran to quench their thirst. The soldier in command lost no time in making it clear who was in control and his expectation for complete submission. After making them stand in a row to make the obligatory bow, they were divided into groups of approximately fifty and housed in coolie huts. There were no beds. Scrounging around, Ivy found an old toothbrush and a quilt. Lining the floor with the quilt, she wrapped the children up and laid them on it. Then, completely exhausted, she and Edna lay on either side of them and squashed like sardines with the other women and children, passed out. The children's cries eventually stirred them from their sleep.

When they awoke, they realised the appalling conditions they had to live in. Not only was there no privacy but there were no toilets and no washing facilities. Neither was there lighting nor furniture.

"Oh, Mum, how can we live like this?" blurted Ivy. "The children …" She stopped short when her mother gave her a warning look – a guard was approaching them.

"Plenty of water," the guard assured, "… drinking only, no washing".

No one dared disobey the order. Before long, the stench from unwashed bodies and the lack of sanitation pervaded the whole camp.

Ivy's hip ached and her leg had swollen up after the long march and she was hardly able to walk. Somehow, she managed to line up for rations: a meagre portion of broken rice, a little sugar, salt and a piece of meat, about the size of a little finger. There was no food other than these rations but plenty of water. Anyone who complained was slapped or kicked, and rations confiscated.

Making watery porridge with the rice, Ivy gave most of her share to Ellen. Jean was still breastfeeding but Ivy had no more milk left and the hungry baby cried in frustration. Ivy comforted her by feeding her the starchy water leftover after boiling rice. In desperation, she began to trade as much of her food as possible for milk and other necessary foods.

The prisoners suffered from malnutrition and harsh treatment. They were frequently slapped across the face, hit with truncheons, or thrown to the ground for any word or movement that was considered an offence to their brutal captors.

Ivy was determined for the family to survive so they would be reunited with their loved ones, one day. She did her best to protect her mother and her girls, and bravely took any assaults on herself. She avoided being slapped or hit too often, by being respectful to her captors.

One day, she tripped and fell while she was queuing for rations, tearing the skin off her shin. To stem the bleeding, she tore a strip from an old rag and wrapped it around her leg. She did not dare ask for help. The wound eventually became infected and would cause her much trouble over the following months.

CHAPTER 9
SINGAPORE FALLS!

Edna and Ivy were unaware the Japanese had already infiltrated the island of Singapore at the time the *Mata Hari* departed with the numerous evacuees. By now, all remaining Allied forces had retreated from Malaya and were on the small island of Singapore. The Causeway was cut from the mainland to hinder the Japanese advancing on the island and the coastline east of the Causeway was strongly defended to prevent the Japanese forces from landing on the island through the small waterways. However, the Japanese attacked the poorly defended north-western coastline and crossed over to the island in collapsible boats. Persistent bombing and amphibious landings from across the Straits of Johore and a hastily repaired Causeway enabled the Japanese to enter what was thought to be an invincible citadel.

In a matter of days, they appropriated crucial public utilities and in doing so, gained control of the water supply of the island. The next morning the Japanese army broke through the British last line of defence. General Arthur Percival had to decide whether to accept defeat or allow the Allied troops to go down fighting. His senior officers had told him that a British counter-attack was no longer possible.

An unconditional surrender to the Japanese was signed on the 15th of February 1942. The British Prime Minister, Winston Churchill, described the fall of Singapore as 'the worst disaster and largest capitulation in British history'.

Singapore was now under Japanese Occupation. The news of the surrender to the Japanese Imperial Army caused widespread bewilderment and disbelief. Although there had been fierce fighting amidst the confusion and chaos in several areas of the island, the shock was the speed at which it was all over and the realisation that they were now under the total control of the Japanese invaders.

Justin's battalion was ordered to assemble at Farrer Park to await instructions from their captors. He was beside himself with worry about Ivy and the family and turned to Kenneth, Ivy's cousin, who was with him, to express his anxiety of not knowing if Ivy and the children had left safely. Justin decided he was going to find out for himself. He left the assembly area, crossed Farrer Park and went to a relative living nearby to ask for some mufti (civilian clothing).

Throwing his army uniform in the nearby Rochor Canal, he hurried to Holly's home where the family had been staying. Upon finding the house empty, he then went to another relative's home and he was told Ivy and family had already left Singapore by ship.

Relieved, Justin raced to his Uncle Charles' house on Bukit Timah Road to see how his mother was. When Charles, who was a Health Officer, returned, he took Justin aside and whispered to him, so his mother would not hear. He informed him that the Japanese were looking for soldiers who had escaped. He urged Justin to report immediately to the Kempeitai, the military secret police of the Imperial Japanese Army. They were known to be ruthless, much like the German Gestapo. Justin reported to the Kempeitai as advised and was marched to the Selarang Barracks at Changi, straight away.

In the days that followed there were indiscriminate killings and massacres of both military personnel and civilians. No one was safe. The local Chinese community was often targeted because of their perceived support for China in the recent Sino-Japanese War. The Allied British troops became Prisoners of War (POWs) and anyone associated with them was interned.

After Justin left Kenneth at the Assembly grounds, the Japanese asked for the Singapore Gunners to identify themselves. Kenneth who absconded soon after Justin's departure, had joined the Gunners as a volunteer but he did not surrender. A few days later, Kenneth was caught while playing cards in a local coffee shop. Coerced into admitting to being an Allied volunteer, he was then escorted to a nearby beach where he was executed.

A short time later, Bill was captured and sent to Selarang Barracks at Changi as well. It was not long before Ralph was apprehended at Holly's house and sent to Changi Prison. He was fifty years old.

Only Jack escaped imprisonment. At 21 years of age, he worked as an Anti-Malarial Inspector. He was given the option to either continue in this role, this time working for the Japanese, or be interned. He would have to go wherever they sent him. Jack agreed to continue his job as he felt he could be of some use to the POWs.

News of the terrible disaster that befell the ships that had left Singapore harbour, filtered into the city. There was already panic and confusion in Singapore at the time. Fires were burning everywhere due to the intense bombardment. Those who heard the news were horrified, particularly those who had loved ones on board the ships. Jack had just been informed of Ralph, Justin, and Bill's imprisonment when snippets of the attack on the ships reached him.

During the weeks at Selarang Barracks, when Bill found out that his father, Ralph, was interned in Changi Prison, he was most concerned for his father's well-being. Bill knew how much his father loved his cigars and as these were impossible to obtain, he saved all his rations of cigarettes for him. He hoped he would get a chance to see his father and help make his imprisonment more tolerable.

He asked permission to see his father and to his surprise was granted a meeting. At the first, father and son hugged each other like they had not seen each other for years. So much had happened in the last couple of months. Then Bill handed over the cigarettes. Ralph could not believe his eyes; how could his son give up smoking at a time of extreme stress and hardship? Bill's generosity overwhelmed him. Up to then, Ralph had focused on Jack, his 'right-hand man' and Ivy, his 'princess'. Though Ralph loved him dearly, he had not given Bill as much consideration.

It struck Ralph that his younger son, a happy, undemanding lad, had grown into a fine young man and a brave one too, putting his life on the line for his country. He now saw Bill's loving and generous nature and was determined to make amends.

"What would you like to do when this war is over, son?" he asked.

"I would like to be a doctor," Bill replied.

Ralph with tears in his eyes and nodding his head, promised, "When we're released, I will help you realise your dream."

After Bill left, Ralph started thinking. Yes, he was aware his son was very bright; the school reports indicated this clearly. However, this was the first time he had learnt of Bill's dream of becoming a doctor. Ralph resolved to spend time getting to know his son better, once the war was over.

Justin and Bill remained in Changi Barracks until October 1942, when they were put on trains and sent to Siam (Thailand). The Japanese were building a railway from Siam to Burma to carry supplies for their forces for an attack on British India. The alternative route was to bring supplies and troops by sea, around the Malay Peninsula but this passage would be too impractical.

The railway project was started in June 1942. For its construction, forced labour was used. The project, referred to as the Burma-Siam Railway was to become known as the infamous Death Railway. Allied POWs and a number of Asian civilians were put to work on building the 415km railway.

In Thailand, Justin and Bill were put in separate camps, just one camp away from each other but they never saw each other again.

Justin and his fellow POWs were made to work in the jungle, hacking a path so the railway line from Bangkok, in the north of Siam to Rangoon in Burma could be built. The railway was built from two points and met at 3 Pagoda Pass.

The men lived in camps set up every 30-50 km along the railway. The POWs at Bill's camp were sent out to work down ravines and slopes to level the ground for railway sleepers to be laid. There, if any man was caught trying to stretch his aching back, he was hit across the shoulders till he fell to the ground. If he could not get up and continue working, he was left on the side of the track without food or water until it was time for his mates to return from work and they helped carry him back to camp.

After landing in Malaya on the 8th of December 1941, the Imperial Japanese Army advanced rapidly sometimes on bicycles.

Japanese armoured units surprised the poorly equipped Allied defenders in the battle of Muar and nearby Bakri.

Some of the fiercest fighting occurred in the defence of Muar and Bakri. The Allies were eventually forced to retreat back to Singapore.

Singapore was heavily bombed by the Japanese prior to the invasion.

Chaotic scenes in Singapore harbour as thousands of British civilians attempted to leave by boat. Ivy and the family had to join a long queue before finally securing passage. Image courtesy of Alamy Stock Photos

The S. S. Mata Hari which Ivy and family boarded in a bid to escape from Singapore.

This map shows the fate of some ships that left Singapore Harbour. The Mata Hari was in the Banka Straits when it was captured. This copyrighted map was kindly supplied by the Malayan Volunteers Group.

British General Arthur Percival (foreground right) signing the unconditional surrender of Singapore on the 15th of February 1942. Sitting across the table was Japanese General Tomoyuki Yamashita (facing camera on the extreme left) and members of his staff.

The fall of Singapore – Japanese soldiers march through the city. It took only 10 weeks from the invasion of Malaya to the fall of Singapore. Image courtesy of AWM

A sketch of Changi Prison in Singapore

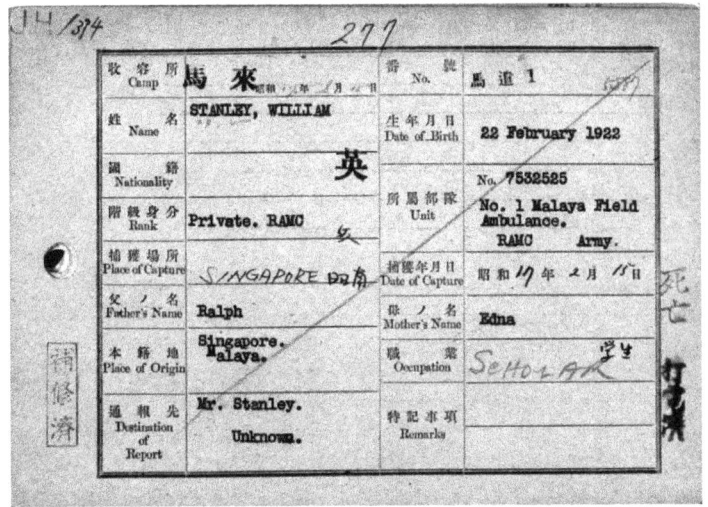

Bill Stanley's POW index card. The reverse side reveals his transfer details from Changi Prison to the infamous Burma-Siam Railway.

POWs labouring on the Burma-Siam Railway. Sickness and the brutal working conditions led to the death of thousands.

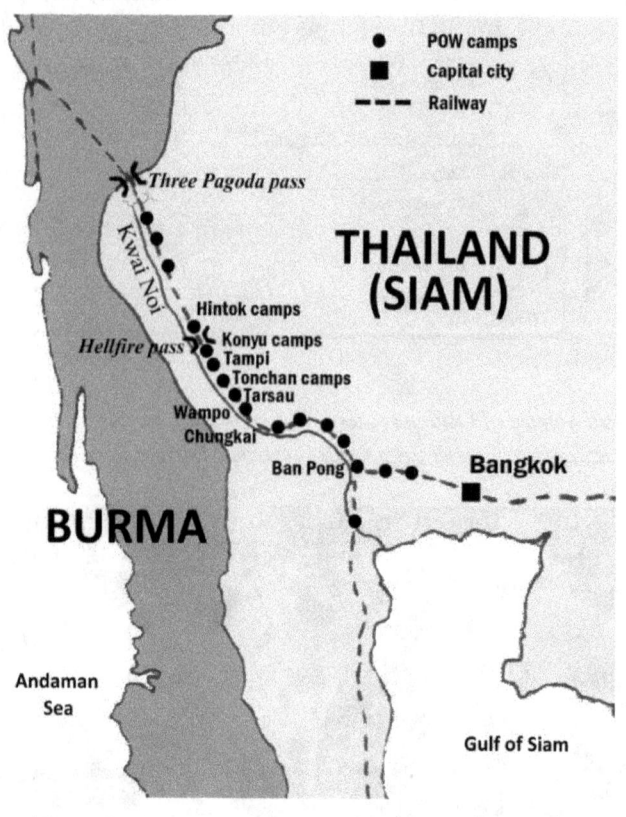

Justin was sent to one of the Tonchan POW camps while Bill was sent to Tampi camp on the Burma-Siam Railway.

CHAPTER 10
THE AGONISING MARCH

Back in Muntok, late in March 1942, the prisoners were told they were being taken to another concentration camp in Palembang, a town on the island of Sumatra, in Indonesia. "Plenty food, plenty food," promised their captors. They were instructed to be ready by three o'clock the next morning to start the march back along the pier. Ivy's leg was very painful; the wound on her ankle was festering and it throbbed uncontrollably.

She was woken from a fitful sleep by shouts and the stomping of heavy boots. It was two in the morning. Ivy gritted her teeth and tried to hurry, knowing the guards would soon arrive. She groped her way in the darkness, wincing in pain, as the others also started to stir. She woke her mother by shaking her shoulder, as she was hard of hearing. Then she gently woke her little daughters, Ellen, not quite two and Jean, barely five months old.

Limping badly, Ivy got her children ready for the journey. The air was cool at that hour of the morning and it had started to drizzle. She wrapped Jean firmly, to prevent her from catching a chill, and tied a nappy over Ellen's head to protect her from the rain.

At least we won't have to walk in the heat of the blazing sun again, she thought. She had just filled a carry bag with nappies, clothes and a bottle of water when they were all ordered to vacate the premises and assemble in the camp grounds. After bowing to their Japanese guards as they had to do every morning and evening at roll call, they were given their rations.

An official announced that they were going to a camp in Palembang. He promised that there would be plenty of food and water when they arrived at their destination. Torches, carried by the guards, dimly lit the road, as the internees made their way back to the pier. As usual, Edna carried Jean in her arms and Ivy led Ellen along by the hand but the little girl was not able to walk for long and began to cry, "Carry, Mummy, carry," raising her arms up towards her mother. Ivy could hardly walk.

With every step she took on the undulating road, littered with loose stones and gravel, sharp stabs of pain would shoot up her affected leg and hip, causing her to cry out. She pulled Ellen along by the hand, but the undernourished child kept stumbling, and lifting her hands up to her mother again, sobbed, "Carry, Mummy, carry, p-l-ease!"

Ivy picked her up with difficulty. Every movement was an effort. She carried her on her left hip, as she had done previously, but her gait was so bad with the limp and the searing pain, she could not keep her balance. She could not carry Ellen astride on her tummy either, because the scar she had from her caesarean-section birth for Jean was still too raw.

Ellen was getting increasingly distressed. Her little legs could not support her any more, and she kept falling. Her knees and hands were bruised from the falls, and her face was streaked with tears and dust from the road. Ivy's heart broke to see her little daughter suffering so.

Ivy's stamina was running out. The pain was driving her to distraction. She looked around desperately for help. Edna was struggling, carrying Jean. It looked as if her mother, who suffered from a heart condition, could collapse at any time. The other prisoners were also having problems marching. Weak from hunger and exhausted from lack of proper sleep, they could hardly keep going; but no one dared stop. The accompanying guards were ever ready to urge them on with their truncheons or bayonets. Those who did fall were abused, prodded and kicked. Being left for dead on the road was the internees' greatest fear. "What am I to do? We'll never survive this journey. Please God, help me," prayed Ivy who was at her wit's end.

An army truck on route to the pier passed by and stopped a short distance in front of her. Ivy saw this as an answer to her desperate prayer. Dragging Ellen along with her, ignoring the child's cries and protestations, Ivy hobbled up to the officer and lifting Ellen up, begged: "Please, please, take my child. She cannot walk." The officer brushed her aside impatiently but Ivy persisted. Showing her inflamed and ghastly swollen leg, she entreated, "I cannot carry her".

The officer wavered, then barked, "You come". Ivy turned to see where Edna and Jean were and was dismayed to see that Edna had lagged some distance behind. Shaking her head, Ivy pointed to her mother and baby and again begged him to take her daughter. The officer waved her away with his hand as the truck started up.

Desperate, Ivy thrust her little girl towards him as the driver pulled out. The officer appeared to hesitate. At that moment, Ivy virtually threw the child at him as the vehicle took off. He grabbed the child by the arm, as Ellen screamed, "Mummy, Mum.-.m-.my ...", her cries ringing in Ivy's ears, long after the truck drove out of sight.

Thinking that she had done the best she could for her child, Ivy wearily joined Edna and Jean again. It was a slow and gruelling march and they were not even halfway to the quay. Suddenly, her relief turned to horror. Snippets of rumours throughout the line came to her confused and wearied mind and with it, the sudden realisation that not all the boats were going to Palembang. Some were destined for Japan or other places. Internees would be shipped off as they arrived at the quay and, as

Ellen would be there long before her family, she could be sent anywhere.

Ivy gave an agonising wail. "What have I done!" she cried. She would never see her daughter again. Ellen was lost. Her child, her beautiful baby was gone, lost forever. Her knees trembled, her legs went limp. She was beside herself.

Then an even more frightening thought entered her mind - the child was screaming as the truck drove down the pier. What if the Japanese officer lost his patience with her? She recalled stories of how babies and children were killed at the whim of the Japanese soldiers.

Ivy became hysterical, crying, wringing her hands in despair, willing her legs to move faster, but to no avail. Step-by-step, the journey never seemed to end and yet fear for her child's safety drove her on. Never, never would she let go of her babies again, no matter what the circumstances, never! But it was too late, Ellen was gone, gone, GONE!!

Guilt, despair and self-recriminations were driving her crazy, but Edna's reassuring presence and comfort gave her the strength to keep going. Edna kept reminding her daughter to trust in God's care as she bravely kept up with her, carrying her baby. After what seemed an eternity, Ivy thought she heard faint cries. They got louder and louder as they came to the end of the long pier. "They're Ellen's cries" Ivy cried to her mother. "I'm sure they are. Please God, let it be her," implored Ivy, as she hobbled and pushed herself forward, frantically searching for her child in the crowd.

Then she saw them – the Japanese officer standing by her inconsolable little daughter. The officer stood, arms folded, feet astride, face stony, seemingly oblivious to the crying child beside him.

Ivy's anguish turned to inexpressible joy. Forgetting her pain and disability, she loped towards her child, who, on seeing her, ran straight into her arms.

"Thank you, thank you," Ivy gasped, looking up at the officer, tears of gratitude streaming down her face. The Officer was furious. His eyes blazed with anger and Ivy instinctively put up her arm to shield herself from the blows she was sure would come.

Instead, he hissed: "Never take baby from mother again," before turning sharply on his heels and marching off.

Ivy never saw that officer again, but she never, ever forgot him and his kindness. She had glimpsed the other face of war.

CHAPTER 11
PALEMBANG

The new destination for the internees was Palembang on the banks of the Moesi River. Palembang was part of the Dutch East Indies on the island of Sumatra. The Japanese had their sights on Palembang, not only for its strategic position but also because it was rich in oil resources with refineries already established and there were two airfields operating in the area as well. The Battle of Palembang raged around the same time as the fall of Singapore and resulted in the Dutch yielding Palembang to Japanese control.

All the prisoners from Muntok were once again put into small boats. The journey took more than a day. It was very uncomfortable and exhausted mothers tried to settle their restless and often agitated children. On arrival, they had to make another arduous walk to a school near the centre of the town. Ivy kept Ellen close to her and suffered the pain of lifting and carrying her with determination. She would never let go of her little girl again.

The internees, particularly the children, were in desperate need of food, which was finally supplied when they reached the school. Men, women and children were all housed together. The conditions were appalling and there was no privacy at all from each other and from the guards. After several days, the men and women were separated and sent to different camps. For an interim period, the female internees and their children stayed in deserted bungalows surrounded by barbed wire. Again, they had to endure the 'watchful eyes' of their guards, who could monitor their every move. One benefit was that Palembang had a hospital run by nuns, The Caritas Catholic Hospital. Those who were sick including Ivy, with her infected leg, obtained the treatment they needed. However, the hospital was eventually closed down in 1943.

It was April 1942 before they were finally settled in their internment camp, known as the Dutch Houses Camp. Dutch women and children living on the island before the war were now taken captive from their homes and forced to join the internees. The captives would refer to the camp as 'Irenelaan' named after the young Dutch princess. Unlike the internees fleeing Singapore on ships, these women had money, personal items and jewellery.

Five families or more were crammed into each dwelling but they had the use of a kitchen. They were given food rations but the amount they received was quite meagre and low in nutritional value, containing hardly any protein. Everyone was dismayed; the hope of 'plenty food' was dashed. Hunger was to continue to be their constant companion. Mothers feared the worst for their little children as they sat in each corner of a room grinding rice to make porridge.

Unlike some of the camps that were run by local administrators, the Dutch Houses camp was directly under Japanese administration. The internees were instructed to go through a similar routine of lining up and bowing to the Officer of the Japanese Imperial Army and flag as they did at Muntok. In a loud authoritative voice, the Officer reminded them that disobedience would not be tolerated. He then continued to lay down the rules. By now, the women, so brow-beaten they didn't dare look at him, just passively accepted whatever he said. They were well acquainted with the severe discipline that would follow any behaviour their captors considered inappropriate.

Ivy kept a very low profile, hoping she and her family would not draw attention. To protect her mother from heavy work, Ivy took over all the chores allocated to Edna as well as her own, like keeping their living space as clean as possible. She had toilet-trained Ellen and was now training Jean. Edna took care of the children and did the cooking. Inadequate food and lack of good hygiene due to a lack of basic necessities such as soap, caused many, especially the children, to fall ill.

Tropical diseases, such as beriberi, dysentery and malaria were always a threat particularly to those already unwell. To supplement what they were given for the young, the women traded food and other items among themselves. They could occasionally buy nutritional food, like eggs and fresh vegetables from local merchants who were allowed into the camp with their bullock carts. Edna and Ivy were severely restricted in their spending, as they had very little left over from the money Justin had given them the last time he saw them. If only they did not have to leave behind the provisions they had purchased with the money.

Ivy was determined to obtain more milk and food for the girls but trading what she could spare from her own rations was not enough. Edna came up with a plan. Edna would use her creativity to produce simple but tasty food and it was then up to Ivy to trade this food in return for milk, or something of value. If successful, not only the children but also the adults would benefit from this enterprise. It was hard work but worth it.

During this time, they kept together as a family, trying to make life as normal as possible for Ellen and Jean. They told stories and sang songs which the girls, especially Ellen, picked up quickly. They never missed saying their prayers and singing the children's favourite hymns before settling them down for the night. One of these hymns was:

Jesus loves me, this I know, for the Bible tells me so
Little ones to him belong; they are weak but He is strong.
Yes, Jesus loves me, Yes, Jesus loves me,
Yes, Jesus loves me, The Bible tells me so.

Ivy also kept their Daddy alive in the children's minds: telling them how brave he was; how much he loved them. "You are a Soldier's Daughter", she would say, "so you must be brave, like your Daddy is brave for you." If either Ellen or Jean got sick or hurt themselves, she would repeat this mantra as she attended to them – hugging and kissing them to give them comfort and reassurance.

One day, a Japanese Official announced that they wanted 'volunteer waitresses' to serve at tables at the Officers' Mess. Ivy volunteered, even though she knew this could result in a dangerous situation for her. The officers could demand that she do more than serve food. Depending on the whims of the officers, she could be subjected to verbal, physical or even sexual abuse.

Ivy shuddered at the thought, but then she considered the advantages the Official enumerated: as volunteers they would be transferred to another section

of the camp; the families would have more space and
better facilities; each volunteer would be paid for a night's
work and in addition, they would be allowed to go
shopping, wearing the 'Enemy-Alien' badge. It meant that
Ivy could buy a few extras for her family. Ivy decided it
was worth the risk and prayed for protection each time
she went on duty.

All the volunteers were taken to work by truck
and they served in a huge hall. They had to stand on two
sides of the hall, and bow low when the Japanese came in.
Ivy never got used to it, the humiliation of bowing to the
enemy. Ivy got on well with the other waitresses and
enjoyed the shopping trips. At last, she could buy milk for
her daughters and other necessities she could afford with
the allowance she was given.

At the mess hall, Ivy kept out of the officers' way
as much as possible, keeping herself busy in the kitchen,
hoping not to be noticed. One day, however, she came
out of the kitchen to find that all the other girls had left
without her. Obviously, they had not noticed she was
missing when they left in the truck. This had never
happened before and the officers were in the hall,
drinking and talking loudly. Ivy panicked!

She dropped whatever she was doing, slipped out of the building as unobtrusively as possible, and ran out to the gates. She was so afraid she would be apprehended, she did not dare go through the main gate. Instead, with her crippled leg, she clamoured over the fence, away from the entrance and tumbled onto the grounds outside the building. Hardly daring to breathe, she expected to be grabbed at any moment but to her amazement, nothing happened. The officers were too drunk to notice and the guard had not seen her. Bruised and cut, she ran as best as she could from the grounds and eventually got back to the camp.

Edna's fellow internees noticed Edna's cooking capabilities. Her preparation of simple but tasty food was a big success and before long she gained a reputation for her culinary skills which reached the ears of the Japanese officials. Edna was given the Cook's job in the Chief Officer's house. To Ivy's relief, she did not have to do waitressing anymore. She continued her trading but no longer needed to use her own rations. In time, she was able to gather and store a small supply of tinned food and other necessities.

Camp life had improved for the family but they remained mindful that the situation could alter dramatically and without warning. Even then, it was a shock when Ellen developed pneumonia. She had a cold and a slight cough which was common among the children. Then suddenly, her temperature went extremely high. She became delirious and her imagination ran riot. "I can see my Daddy," she kept saying. "Oh Mummy, let's go see Daddy." With the Catholic Hospital closed, there was no medical treatment available, Ivy anxiously tried to keep her temperature down with wet towelling.

Edna, taking a bag of rice she had been given to make porridge, boiled some of the rice and putting it between two napkins, used it as a poultice on her granddaughter's chest. Hours passed with Ivy and Edna taking turns to be at Ellen's side, attending to her needs. Finally, Ellen's temperature broke and she fell into a peaceful sleep. For Ivy and Edna, no words could describe their joy.

After a few days, Ellen was well again.

That night Edna and Ivy knelt in prayer to give thanks to the Lord. Ivy fell off to sleep straight after, mainly from exhaustion but not Edna. Memories of her childhood came flooding back to her. She was the eighth of ten children and she remembered her confusion and distress when, as a small child her father, Tom Miles drove her and her youngest sister, Mavis to a Convent and left them there with the nuns. Edna was vaguely aware of having a mother but she was not around anymore.

As she grew older, Edna learned that her mother, Eleanor, had gone to England where she ran a millinery business in Bond Street, London. She had remarried a Mr Schneider. As a single father, Tom probably thought the Convent was the best place for the two young girls to be looked after and receive an education at the same time.

Tom, who came from a long line of seafarers, worked for a Shipping line. He was renowned as a chess player in South-East Asia and became chess champion of the region. One of his sons, Cuthbert, known as Bertie, would follow the family tradition and love of the sea by becoming a ship's engineer.

Life in the convent was tough; the nuns were strict and punished any behaviour they considered unacceptable, even innocuous things like bed wetting. Besides her studies, she was also taught to cook and sew her own clothes. During her time at the convent, Edna learned to pray and she developed a strong faith.

When she approached her teen years, her father brought her home. In her mind, Edna could see herself in her father's house. He was a very strict man. She had learnt to read at school but she had not reached a level her father considered appropriate for her age. He took over that part of her education by getting her to read the newspapers. She quickly became adept in reading and writing. She also acquired all the other graces necessary to become an accomplished young woman.

Edna finally fell asleep grateful for her upbringing. The strict and disciplined years of her youth now helped her to cope with her present circumstances and provide Ivy with the support she needed in this harsh environment.

CHAPTER 12
THE STANLEY BROTHERS

Jack was determined to find out the fate of various members of the family. His position as a Health Inspector working in an anti-malarial unit for the Japanese gave him an advantage when making enquiries. He could travel around Singapore relatively freely and could visit relevant authorities as well as friends and family at times. After several months, he learned that his mother, sister, and her children had survived the ordeal of the bombing of the evacuee ships heading for safe havens. They were captured and interned in one of the Japanese camps in the Dutch East Indies, now known as Indonesia.

He then tried to find a way to bring them back home to Malaya. With patience and determination, he persisted in his quest. A breakthrough came when he was told he could sponsor Edna, Ivy and his nieces back to Singapore through the Red Cross. The fact that they had relatives in Singapore made them eligible for sponsorship. However, success would depend on the approval of the Officer-in-Charge of their Camp.

After completing his work in Singapore, the Japanese authorities sent Jack to prisoner-of-war camps along the Burma-Siam Railway. He was to continue his work of diagnosing malaria through the microscopic examination of blood from POWs and their Japanese captors. Malaria, most common in tropical regions, is a serious mosquito-borne illness that can be fatal if not treated, especially when there are complications. The severity of complications depends on how the disease spreads within the infected patient.

There were several camps along the railway and Jack was kept busy moving from one camp to another. Throughout the camps, he saw the appalling living conditions inflicted on POWs. Many of the prisoners had developed tropical ulcers, which often became infected.

Severe malnutrition and inadequate medical supplies restricted the healing of ulcers, which could erode muscles, tendons and even bone. In addition, exhaustion from overwork and harsh punitive treatment made the men more vulnerable to diseases like malaria, dysentery and cholera. Jack noticed many of the POWs had to contend with more than one health issue.

One day, while Jack was examining some blood slides from prisoners, he came across his own brother's name. It was a relief to know Bill was still alive. Jack had been on a constant look-out for names of family and friends.

He proceeded with his examination of Bill's slide. As he studied it carefully it became evident Bill had succumbed to malaria. He was determined to get in contact with him. The main hurdle was Jack's guard, a Japanese soldier who was given strict orders to shoot Jack, should he step out of line in any way. Jack was well-aware of his tenuous position when he was seconded to work for the Japanese. He would be treated well if he did as he was told, otherwise, it would end badly for him. Jack already had a good relationship with his guard because he treated him with respect, rather than as an enemy to be feared.

Now he had to gain the guard's trust if he was to have any hope of seeing Bill. He managed to convince the guard that he was trustworthy and the guard agreed to turn a blind eye to Jack's efforts to locate his brother. There was an understanding that if anything went wrong or caused suspicion, the guard, to protect himself, would shoot Jack immediately.

With this arrangement in place, Jack managed to speak to some of the POWs in Bill's camp and asked them to pass on a message to Bill. He also organised for POW clothing to be smuggled to him. Bill, a medic in the army, was much loved by his fellow POWs. In the camp, he was well known for his kindness and untiring efforts to relieve the pain and suffering of the sick where possible. Now his comrades were willing to put their lives at risk to reunite him and his brother.

The two brothers were overjoyed to see each other again and cherished the few meetings they had over the following couple of weeks. During these times, Bill poured out his heart to his 'big brother' and expressed the fear that his family would never know what had become of him.

As a medic, he knew he was seriously ill. He spoke of the brutality of the Korean guards and their Japanese commanders. He spoke of how his fellow POWs helped each other, even when they were suffering themselves from hunger, sickness and pain. Bill's eyes lit up when he described the camaraderie among his mates which kept them going day by day, and how it created 'a very special bond' which made them steadfastly loyal to one another.

Jack listened quietly. What Bill was talking about, he knew was true; he had witnessed similar situations. He comforted and consoled his brother the best way he could then tried to lift Bill's spirits by recalling happier times they had spent as boys and young men. He generally succeeded. Jack gave Bill the good news of how he managed to arrange for their mother, Ivy and the children to be released from internment and be returned to Singapore. He felt there was no point in telling Bill that it was conditional on obtaining permission from the Japanese Officer-in-charge. The relieved look on Bill's face affirmed his decision. He confirmed that their father, Ralph, was still in Changi Prison, at least when he saw him last and Jack reassured Bill that their father was coping with internment.

At one of their meetings, Jack carefully broke the news that he was in love with Millie and was hoping to marry her. Over the last couple of years, he had become close to her and from there, love had blossomed.

Bill had started casually dating Millie before the war and now Jack, feeling a little apprehensive, hoped this news would not upset his brother. Instead, Bill congratulated him and said, "I would love to be at your wedding as your Best Man but I know it will not be possible." Jack just hugged his brother, too emotional to say anything. As Jack was leaving, Bill, thinking aloud, expressed his desire to write home to the family. He quickly recanted, "It would be too dangerous, how can I even think of it," and let the suggestion drop.

On his next visit, Jack quietly handed over writing materials to Bill, assuring him it was fine for him to write. He knew that writing to family meant a great deal to Bill. At their next meeting, Bill secretly slipped two sealed envelopes into Jack's hands, whispering that one was for his mother and Ivy. Jack noticed the second envelope was addressed to Millie. "This is for her, Jack," and grasping his hand, said, "I wish you both all the best. Give her a hug from me." Jack nodded, quietly putting the letters in his pocket. He was taking a huge risk, for if he was found with them he would be almost certainly shot.

Shortly after Bill wrote these letters, one of the POWs in the camp passed Jack an urgent message. Bill had collapsed. Only a week or so earlier, Bill was doing all he could to help his mates who were critically ill, even putting wet packs on their foreheads to cool down their temperature. When Jack arrived, Bill was in a coma, the final stages of cerebral malaria. It was the most serious complication of malaria, where in a matter of days, the affected person could go from a severe infection to a coma and then death.

He spoke softly to his brother while stroking his hand. It pained Jack that he had to go back to work rather than stay by Bill's side. It was even harder to keep his emotions in check when at work, otherwise he would have given himself away. Bill slipped away peacefully that night. Jack was given the news just before the POWs reported to the Japanese Officer-in-charge that another of their mates had passed away. They were told to bury him like they did the others who had died.

His mates begged Jack to let them have all of Bill's clothes and his boots. Such items were precious in the camps. Jack agreed without hesitation. When Jack sneaked back before Bill's body could be taken away, he brought his hockey shirt with him so his brother could be buried in it. Jack had participated in interstate hockey matches in Malaya and Singapore. When the Japanese took control and he was sent to the Burma-Siam Railway, Jack decided to pack a hockey shirt to help him recall the happier days before the war. Now he felt better that his beloved brother would have a more dignified burial.

Sometime later, Jack was on his way to his next designated camp to continue his work. While having a break near a river, he heard his name called, "Jack" in a low voice. He turned around and was surprised to see his brother-in-law, Justin who was returning to his camp. It was just one camp away from the one where Bill had been interned. At first, Jack did not recognise Justin – he was so thin and dark from constant exposure to the sun.

The men had to hide their joy at meeting each other, as Jack's guard was not far away chatting to the other guards. However, Jack managed to tell Justin that Ivy and the children had been captured at sea following their escape from Singapore and they had been interned in Sumatra. But he was also able to tell Justin that he believed they were soon to be transferred back to Singapore.

Justin's initial reaction was one of relief, then he could barely contain himself with joy. He enthusiastically thanked Jack for the wonderful news. He explained how he had at first thought his family had escaped safely but when he heard of the disaster that befell the ships and contradictory rumours about the fate of the evacuees aboard, he thought he was going to lose his mind.

Jack then gave Justin the sad news of Bill's death. Justin told him he had just heard the news. He explained that his tooth was giving him a great deal of pain, making it difficult for him to carry out his duties, so, with permission, he went by barge to Bill's camp for treatment. He was hoping to catch up with Bill, as he had not seen him since they were together in Selarang Barracks, Changi, in Singapore.

From a few of his mates who had been treated at Bill's medical camp, Justin knew that Bill was there and how much he was appreciated for his work. Before returning to his camp, he looked for Bill but could not find him. Luckily, he met a mutual friend who sadly informed him that Bill had recently died. When Jack whispered that he was carrying a couple of Bill's letters to take back to Singapore, Justin immediately asked him if he could also take back a letter to Ivy, which he did.

CHAPTER 13
RETURN TO SINGAPORE

After eighteen months of internment, Edna and Ivy along with a few other internees received news that there was a possibility that they may be sent back to Singapore. At first, they refused to believe it, thinking it was just a cruel joke. When they were informed that one of their relatives had approached the Red Cross offering to be a sponsor for them to return, they were ecstatic with joy. However, there was one condition. The Chief Officer at the camp had to give his approval. Each family or individual had to put a strong case forward before he would give his consent. Ivy, with Jean on her arm, made her desperate plea for her family to be sent back to Singapore. Her request was granted.

In the latter part of 1943, Ivy, Edna and the girls boarded a Japanese ship bound for Singapore. There were tears of happiness, joy and prayers of gratitude as they stepped on board. The journey, however, was harrowing with the internees crammed into the bowels of the ship. Despite this, as they approached the harbour, Ivy could hardly contain herself with excitement. She scanned the pier for Justin and Jack, but neither of them was there to meet the weary but relieved little family. Instead, Edna's sister, Inez, was waiting for them. Feeling puzzled and deeply disappointed, Ivy tried hard to hold back her tears as she greeted her aunt.

As they were driven to her home in a taxi she told them that Jack was their sponsor but he had been transferred to the Burma-Siam border just before they were due to arrive. Feeling confused, Edna asked the reason for the transfer and was told that their Japanese captors had seconded Jack to work in the Health area which included the Burma-Siam camps. Inez also broke the news that Ralph was captured and was interned in

Changi Prison. Bill too was taken prisoner when his battalion was seized.

"But where's Justin?" cried Ivy. "Where is my husband?" fear striking her breast. Ivy sobbed her heart out when she was told Justin had also been captured. Both Justin and Bill were initially sent to Changi Barracks but were later transported to the Burma-Siam border to work on the infamous Death Railway. Inez also told them of the horror and hardship during the fall of Singapore and its repercussions to the local population and their families.

Inez invited them to live with her. She informed them that despite the Japanese occupation of the country, the family were free to travel within the island. A Japanese Officer would periodically check that they were adhering to the curfew rules. As soon as they settled in, they applied for permission to visit Ralph. Permission was granted for either Edna or Ivy to visit Ralph in Changi Prison once a month and they decided to alternate their visits.

Ivy was the first to visit Ralph. It was an emotional reunion. "You are all alive, my darling! Thank God," Ralph exclaimed. "How is Mummy? Is she alright?

How is she coping? I've missed her so." Ivy reassured her father that her mother was coping, but was starting to feel the strain. She conveyed his wife's love and explained that they had to take turns to visit him. She had come first to make sure he was all right. Her mother had missed him terribly and had been praying for him morning and night. She could not wait to see him the following month.

"But how are you, Papa?" asked Ivy as she shed tears of joy and relief that Ralph was still alive, but also tears of sadness and fear when she saw how emaciated Ralph was. She shuddered at the thought of what he had gone through, knowing how brutal his captors could be.

They spent the next few precious minutes they had, speaking about his granddaughters, Ellen and Jean. In a tender voice, Ivy described how the girls were growing up and that their survival was a miracle. Then she spoke about the starvation, disease and the terrible conditions they had to endure. "Mummy's been so wonderful, Papa. I thought I would have to look after her; instead, she has looked after all of us. I wouldn't have managed without her," said Ivy, a catch in the voice.

Ralph nodded and putting his arm around her, said, "I understand, darling. Mummy may not be robust in health but she has amazing inner strength." They said their goodbyes, happy to know they would see each other again soon. Ivy went home to relieve Edna's mind that her beloved husband was managing in prison.

They now had to adjust to living in 'relative' freedom again. In the next few days, while Edna was having a much-needed rest, Ivy met up with some relatives and friends who had not been interned. In one of their conversations, Ivy was surprised to learn from her friends that it was possible to send letters to POWs through the Red Cross. Filled with hope, she immediately set about writing to her husband and her younger brother Bill, with an outpouring of emotion, having not seen or heard from them for more than a year. Once the letters were completed she immediately hired a trishaw to take her to the Red Cross Headquarters where she organised for her letters to be sent. Soon after returning from the Red Cross, a Japanese soldier was at the door.

"You," pointing his finger threateningly at her face, "Kempeitai Headquarters. Tomorrow morning 10 o'clock."

It suddenly dawned on Ivy that one of the conditions of their detention was not to write to anyone.

In her highly emotional state on hearing the news of her husband, father, and brothers' fate, Ivy inadvertently violated the terms of their repatriation. Ivy and Edna could not sleep that night as they were so afraid. They knelt and prayed that nothing terrible would happen to them or the family. The next morning, Ivy reported to the Kempeitai.

"Where your husband?" the Officer demanded. Trying hard to keep calm, Ivy replied that he was a prisoner-of-war. "Where your father?" was the next question he fired at her. In a shaky voice, she answered that he was in Changi Prison. "Then you go too. You go prison for writing this," he shouted, waving her letters in front of her. "Get ready one o'clock tomorrow. Truck pick you up."

Ivy cried and pleaded not to be interned again, but to no avail.

Edna was very supportive when Ivy returned home from the Kempeitai still crying. Edna had a strong faith and trusted that God would help them in their new predicament. She tried to console Ivy by saying that at least they may have a chance of seeing Ralph more often. They got their things together and were ready when the truck came the next day. As they boarded the truck, Ivy smiled for the first time that day. Many of the detainees who had returned to Singapore with them on the ship were already in the truck. At least they would be among friends in Changi Prison.

CHAPTER 14
CHANGI PRISON

Changi Prison was initially built in the 1930's by the British as a 'model' prison, with features such as electric lights, hot water and flushing toilets designed for 600 inmates. However, by 1942 the Japanese had crammed between two to three thousand civilian POWs into the jail thereby straining the capacity for sanitation and function. In the meantime, the military POWs were held nearby at Selarang Barracks.

When they arrived at Changi Prison, the new internees were taken to their cells in the Women and Children's Wing of the building. As they entered the building, Edna and Ivy were surprised and relieved to see a familiar face, Mrs Milne, the Headmistress of the Government Primary School in Muar where Roy, Justin's brother, had been teaching. She had been interned because she was English.

A minimum of four people was allotted to a one-person cell and as Ivy's family consisted of four members, they were given a cell to themselves. It had a cement slab for a bed. Ivy scavenged around for things to use as bedding and blankets to make the cell more comfortable. Despite there being a toilet in each cell the smell was overpowering and diseases like dysentery, which were rampant throughout the prison, were a real threat. Bed bugs infested the bedding while mosquitoes continually buzzed and hovered. There was a constant threat of contracting malaria. Ivy ensured mosquito nets protected the children when sleeping, while she and Edna prayed they would not be affected as there were not enough of mosquito nets for everyone. Malaria and dysentery cases were treated at the hospital, however many died from these diseases due to malnutrition, poor sanitation, and the lack of supplies and resources. Ivy made a determined effort to keep their little cell as meticulously clean as possible.

A few days after Ivy's arrival at Changi Prison, Mrs Milne took Ivy into the ironically named "Rose Garden", where not a single plant nor even a blade of grass grew. It was there that she told Ivy about the massacre of her relatives in Ulu Tiram which was thirteen miles from the Malayan town of Johore Bahru.

On the 14th of March 1942, they were part of a large group of Eurasians who had chosen to go to a rubber estate to escape the invading Japanese but were found a short time later by Japanese soldiers. Rev. Fr. Louis Ashness, Justin's youngest brother, Osie and another relative, Stenny, had cycled to Ulu Tiram to deliver food supplies to the camp only to find evidence of a recent massacre. Each and everyone in this party of Eurasians had been executed, then pushed into freshly dug graves.

Ivy was horrified and distressed to hear of the Ulu Tiram massacre; so many of her relatives gone and to think that Edna, herself, and the children very nearly went there with them. Ivy wept as memories of the happy times she and her cousins had together came flooding back. Her mother would have to be told the tragic news of what happened to close family members and Ivy worried how she would react.

After a while, when Ivy regained her composure, Mrs Milne gently continued. She told Ivy that at nearby Taman Mount Austin, Justin's brother Roy, his wife Belle and daughter Angela were with another group of Eurasians. Roy and the other men were rounded up and made to leave to register at the Johore Civil Service Club. The women and children were put into groups and Roy's wife and daughter were in the final lot to be executed. They were all tied up and were just about to be bayonetted when a little girl amongst the group began to cry. The Japanese Officer suddenly changed his mind and gave the command not to kill. He then had them untied and told them to stay where they were and he would be back the next day. A few locals who witnessed the massacre raised the alarm and Fr. Louis Ashness who knew someone in authority managed to obtain a pass and acted swiftly. He arrived very early next morning and whisked the survivors of the group to safety.

In Changi Prison, everyone found their own way to survive and cope with internment. Some people socialised by joining in groups such as playing cards or engaging in other activities, as it was a means to relieve the boredom and stress of their situation. Others chose to become more reclusive or insular, putting up a defensive wall to maintain control of their lives by shutting out others. In Ivy's case, she decided that to survive this ordeal with her precious family, she would focus all her energy on the things she needed to do to keep the family safe and healthy.

The door to their cell could not be locked, but Ivy managed to secure it with a short stick. One day, Jean accidentally locked herself in the cell and did not seem to understand as Ivy and Edna tried to tell her how to unlock it. Ivy tried to explain to Jean how to hold the door and pull out the stick. "Pull hard, darling, you can do it," Ivy urged, doing her best to coax her to pull harder. Initially, Jean tried to do so but she soon lost interest and just walked around in the cell, singing to herself. In desperation, Ivy appealed to the internee who was In-Charge of the Women's section for help. After a couple of hours, Jean was finally coaxed to pull out the stick.

Years later when Ivy was speaking to friends and recalling her time during her internment, she said that life in Changi Prison was better than at the other camps. There were electric lights and hot water and the internees had a little more freedom. Although at times they were not allowed to gather in groups or talk, at other times they could hold concerts and were even able to exchange parcels with the men. But they were forbidden to speak to the men, which was so frustrating.

One of the cleaning jobs allocated to the women was to pick up the garbage bins from around the jail and take them out to the collection area. The civilian male internees would come and collect the bins, take them away to be emptied and then bring them back. The passage they had to go through had an open grill and it gave the women a chance to see their menfolk. In this way, Edna and Ivy occasionally would see Ralph but they had to be very careful not to be seen communicating with him. Those who were caught talking or signalling to the men were punished.

Besides having the opportunity of seeing their menfolk on garbage clearing days, the women were also able to communicate with the men through what was called the "Secret Service Message". One of the walls of their section of the prison was adjacent to the men's section and almost every night letters would be passed between male and female internees. Whispered messages would occur when there was a distracting noise or singing. In this way, many a romance developed. An example of such a romance, was between Ivy's friend Amelia and Tom, one of the internees who carried in the food rations for the women's section.

The relationship between Amelia and Tom appeared to be going along fine until Amelia became more attracted to someone else and she abruptly broke off her relationship with him. Tom was devastated and threatened to commit suicide. Amelia, not expecting such a reaction, appealed to Ivy to help her. Reluctantly Ivy agreed to write to him as a friend of Amelia's, but only as a pen-pal. At Christmas, the men managed to smuggle presents to the women, using the truck that delivered food supplies to the prison. Some of the items included coconuts with faces drawn on them. Ivy was amazed when she received a gold watch from this man, thanking her for her kindness.

The female internees thought of ingenious ways of contacting and trading with the men. One of the secret exchanges between them was when one of the internees died at the prison. The men had to take the coffin to the burial place, bury the body, and bring the empty coffin back. Unbeknown to their captors, the coffin was often filled with a form of brown sugar, known as *gula-malaka*, and all those who had money would buy. For Ivy and Edna, the sugar was a treat they could not resist for the family.

Then something happened that would shake the male internees in Changi Prison to the core and send a ripple of fear through the women's camp also. The Double Tenth incident occurred on the 10th of October 1943. There had been a raid on Singapore Harbour and seven Japanese ships were sunk. The Japanese did not know who had carried out the attack, but strongly suspected several of the civilian internees at Changi Prison, including Ralph, as well as some of the local population. They were accused of having self-made secret radios and giving out information about their ships. Ralph and fifty-six Changi prisoners were rounded up and taken away to be interrogated and tortured.

When the news reached Edna and Ivy, they were deeply upset and terrified of what could happen to Ralph. There were rumours that some prisoners were put on top of the tower and left to dry out in the sun. Many of the men taken, never returned. The Japanese believed there was a 'Stanley' sending out messages to the Allies, so Ralph, who was a 'Stanley' and a Dr Stanley, became the focus of intense questioning and examination. Ivy and Edna prayed. Ralph was away for a week before finally being sent back to his cell. He was in such a state when he came back that he could not even walk. Ralph and the others who were released were so weakened by their ordeal, they were administered whatever medicines and vitamins that were available in the camp infirmary.

Edna and Ivy were given permission to visit Ralph once a week. On the day of their first visit, they were shocked to see the state he was in. Ralph told them, in a voice that was still shaky, how waiting for his turn to be tortured was agony but finally, they took Dr Stanley with them and left him alone. Dr Stanley was never seen again. This horrendous experience Ralph underwent left him both a physical and emotional wreck for a long time.

It was learned later on, the Japanese had assumed there had been intelligence and information emanating from Changi Prison which enabled the attack on their ships in Singapore Harbour. In fact, Australian commandos had conducted the raid, independent of those incarcerated at Changi Prison. None of the local civilians in Singapore were involved.

CHAPTER 15
ON WINGS OF SONG

The internees were feeling nervous and apprehensive after the Double Tenth incident. The mood, in general, was sober and many were restless. To allay the agitation obviously present in the prison community, the Japanese officials decided that male internees could volunteer to take children for a walk around the jail courtyard. Ellen loved these visits. She would come back from these walks full of stories of her Daddy, her imagination running wild. One day, she came running in with some wild flowers in her hand, "Mummy, Mummy, Daddy gave these for you".

Ivy's heart would break every time Ellen mentioned her father and whenever she asked for something Ivy could not give or do, she would say, 'Wait until your Daddy comes." Ellen believed this and was quite content to wait.

As Ellen grew older, she had to attend the *tenko*, meaning roll call, where she would stand with the other women every morning and evening and bow low to their captors as they strutted past them. If anyone did not bow low enough for their satisfaction, she was struck with a baton or kicked on the bottom. If the officer was in a bad mood, the offender would feel the tip of the bayonet pressed in her back. "Bow!" came the gruff order.

Ellen was so terrified of being hit that she often bent over until she nearly fell.

There were many children in Changi Prison. Like Ellen and Jean, they were undernourished and prone to disease. They also missed out on formal schooling, although some lessons were organised for the older children. Their experience in prison deeply affected them and they spent their days trying to entertain themselves, playing games, chasing each other and at times even bullying each other.

Ellen, with her vivid imagination, would sometimes make up stories in her head and happily play by herself, unaware of those around her. On one occasion, this made her a target for bullying from a couple of boys in the jail. As she was easily startled and shy in nature, she quickly burst into tears, which encouraged the bullying behaviour to continue.

On seeing what was happening, Jean quietly came from behind and using her best weapon to defend her sister, bit the main bully on the arm. He screamed in pain and immediately ran away. Though small, Jean was fierce and quick to attack and took on a protective role for her sister. Very quickly the bullying ceased.

Jean herself was never bullied.

Ivy taught the girls, especially Ellen, who was older, her spelling and times-tables. The children learned their prayers and the little hymns Edna often sang. Whenever either of the girls fell and hurt themselves or were afraid, Ivy would remind them to be brave like their Daddy. She kept Justin alive in their thoughts and lives and made them courageous and strong by using their father as an example.

She even wrote a special song for them to learn and sing to their Daddy when the family was together again. Using a popular Indonesian style song, a 'Kronchong' for the melody, she wrote the lyrics:

TO MY DADDY

There's a tear in my eye, Daddy,
And a pain in my heart here too
For I'm longing to see you Daddy,
And mother's been waiting for you.
But years have come and years have gone,
Still there's no message from you
Do you wonder why, there's a tear in my eye,
When I think of you?
If there could come, but a message,
Written and signed, Dad, by you
I would be so happy to see
My Daddy's been thinking of me
Mother says, as she holds my hand,
Child, understand, your Daddy is grand
You should be as proud as can be,
For your Daddy is brave dear, for you.

After more than two years of internment, there was no communication between Ivy and Justin. They did not even know if the other was alive or dead. As well as letters, radios and newspapers were forbidden which made the internees feel very isolated. This, Ivy found hard to bear. In the evenings, although exhausted, Ivy wrote poems, love songs and letters to her beloved husband, hoping to give them to him one day. This is one of the songs she composed for him:

TILL I SEE YOUR FACE ONE DAY

At the close of day, when my work is through
And it's time to kneel and pray
My thoughts go out to you.
It is then I feel, Oh, so lonesome and blue
And long with each sigh of mine
That I was once again with you.

Oh, how my heart is aching
And how the tear-drops long to start
But with the crowd that's always round me
I try to hide my breaking heart.

Just how long will it be,
When you can come back to me?

I will never cease to pray,
That I will see your face some day.

Jack continued his work in Thailand on the Burma-Siam Railway until early 1944 when he was ordered to return to Singapore. On his journey home, he made a detour by catching a taxi from Segamat, the closest railway station to Muar where his sweetheart Millie lived. He immediately went to Millie's family home and after the joyous greetings, gave her and the family the sad news about Bill. He then quietly handed Bill's letter to Millie.

As soon as the opportunity arose, Jack drew Millie aside and proposed to her. To his delight, she accepted his proposal without hesitation. Millie then opened Bill's letter with Jack at her side. They cried with bittersweet tears of happiness when Bill cheekily wrote, "You naughty girl, you could not wait for me, you had to fall in love with my brother, the lucky fellow. I wish you both all happiness."

It was a shock for Jack to learn that his mother, Edna, his sister Ivy and her children had been re-interned. As soon as he arrived in Singapore, Jack reported in at the Japanese headquarters. He then sought and was granted permission to visit Edna and Ivy in Changi Prison. It was a wonderful reunion and a great relief for them to know Jack was alive and well. They had been waiting for his return, alternating between hope and fear for his safety.

When he gave them the news of Justin and their meeting on the Burma-Siam Railway, Ivy was elated. She was so happy to know he was alive it brought tears to her eyes. Jack then put his arms gently around his mother as he broke the news that Bill had died. As he began to tell her, Edna's eyes pleaded with him to say anything different to what she knew he was about to reveal. They all grieved together for Bill, their beloved son and brother. The fact that Jack had found Bill and could spend quality time together with him in those last days, brought enormous consolation to Edna and Ivy. Edna's thoughts turned to Ralph and how he would cope with the news. Jack had permission to visit Ralph the next day and reassured Edna he would do his best to comfort his father once breaking the sad news.

Jack then gave them the letters from Bill and Justin. Edna and Ivy could not believe their eyes. They could not thank him enough for risking his life to bring Bill and Justin's letters to them.

After not hearing from Justin for many years, it was wonderful for Ivy to get secret letters from him. There were two letters – one, hastily written after he met Jack in Thailand and the other, a beautiful love letter which ended with a song he had penned for her.

Edna's letter from Bill was also addressed to Ralph and Ivy. It was a very touching letter telling them how much he loved them and missed them. He wrote about the incredible joy of seeing his brother again and the happy memories it brought back at a time when things could not have been worse.

Bill also described what had been happening to him and his fellow POWs in a separate letter he had written long before the brothers met. It was heartbreaking to read but Edna and Ivy were comforted to know that Jack had spent time with his brother before he passed away and that he was there to bury him when the time came.

Before leaving Jack had some good news to give to Edna and Ivy. With a big grin on his face, he announced that he and Millie were engaged. They planned to marry on the 3rd of June 1944, that same year. Edna and Ivy were so happy for Jack and asked him to convey their best wishes to Millie, saying, "We wish you both all God's blessings for a long and happy life." They were disappointed they could not be at the wedding but understood the happy couple did not want to wait, as life during wartime was so unpredictable, you took your chances when they presented.

After Jack left, Edna and Ivy read and re-read their letters several times more. And yet, they were so afraid the letters would be found on them in Changi Prison and that they may also incriminate Jack, they reluctantly destroyed them that night, a decision, however wise, they both regretted in later years. However, before parting with her precious letter, Ivy first cut out and kept the song Justin had written her:

'TIL YOU RETURN TO ME

Under a cloak of gaiety,
I hide a secret pain.

My heart is ever waiting,
Must it wait just in vain?
I will never forget the day
The day we said "Good-Bye"
The tears that welled in your eyes,
The parting look, the sigh.
'Twas cruel fate that parted us
Our misery to see
My heart will ever lonesome be,
'Til you return to me.

CHAPTER 16
SIME ROAD CAMP

In the latter part of 1944, the internees at Changi Prison were told they were going to a place called Sime Road Camp a few miles away from the prison.

At the new camp, they would be accommodated in houses again instead of prison cells. The male civilian internees had already been transferred to this camp. However, when Ivy and Edna arrived, they found there was already a very large number of both male and female internees from the various POW camps located outside Singapore, now living there. Although living in the same camp, the Japanese strictly enforced segregation of the men from the women and children, keeping them in separate compounds.

Soon after Ivy, Edna and the girls arrived, a new batch of internees was transferred to the camp. One of them was Ivy's young cousin, Barbara, whom Ivy took under her wing. They were housed in *attap* huts, which had bamboo frames and thatched roofs made from leaves of the Nipa Palm. POWs had recently built them to accommodate the large influx of internees. Each hut had twelve compartments. Barbara (Babsie) joined Edna, Ivy and the girls in Hut 12, Compartment 4.

Besides doing their routine chores, the women were responsible for planting and maintaining the vegetable gardens, while the male internees were allocated tasks frequently involving heavy physical work. In the camp, the internees received rations which were meagre, although the men were permitted to do some shopping from traders who were allowed access to the camp. Despite the segregation of the men from the women and children, covert bartering between them meant the women could obtain some of the essential ingredients and items required for cooking and good hygiene.

Each of the huts was equipped with a communal kitchen which included a stove. The women had to take turns to use the stove. Ivy always remained in the background, but an incident over the stove would show the other women of the camp that Ivy, though quiet and unobtrusive, was not meek and docile. There was a domineering internee who tended to monopolise the stove. She would curtly say to Ivy whenever she tried to do some cooking, "There's no room. Come back later." This went on for days and when Ivy put a pot of potatoes on the stove anyway, she pushed it away, saying rudely, "I told you there is no room."

This tension finally precipitated in a confrontation between Ivy and her nemesis on one of these occasions. Ivy said to her, "I have to use this stove just like you and the others. You're not going to stop me. My children have to eat."

"Oh yeah?" sneered the internee, coming up close to Ivy's face. "I'll knock your teeth in first," and shook her fist at Ivy threateningly. She was a large woman unlike Ivy, who was relatively petite.

Ivy retreated. That night she decided she simply had to do something if she and her family were not to be intimidated. The next day Ivy went to the kitchen and saw that the woman had a pot of hot oil on the stove. Ivy took the pot and facing her with the pot in her hand, said in a loud voice, "I don't think you've had an oil bath for a long time. Don't you ever threaten to knock my teeth in again. I dare you to come near me." The look in Ivy's eyes told the tormentor that she had met her match in this small woman. A couple of other women were in the kitchen at the time and they were stunned at the stand-off. That was the last time Ivy had trouble from the kitchen bully or anyone else.

Life in the camp settled down for Ivy and the family as they adapted to their new surroundings. At one stage, the internees were told they would be allowed to meet their relatives and friends in the garden on certain allocated days. Ivy and Edna were overjoyed at the thought they could finally see Ralph. However, this privilege was revoked almost immediately, much to everyone's disappointment. Some of the guards complained to the Japanese Commandant that the internees were stealing potatoes from the vegetable garden. At the same time, two teenaged girls were caught climbing papaya trees in the camp to steal the fruit. As punishment, the girls were forced to stand in the hot sun, with no water, from morning to night. Small incidents like these could change the whole mood of the camp as the internees struggled through the months of internment.

In some ways, life at Sime Road camp was better than Changi Prison. The men and women had a little more freedom and could spend time outdoors. But the years of incarceration and deprivation had taken a toll on the internees. Several men, women and children died at the Sime Road Camp either from malnutrition or disease, particularly malaria.

One day in August 1945 the internees suddenly found themselves left alone; the Japanese soldiers and the guards seemed to have disappeared overnight. Rumours swept around the camp that the war was ending and that they would be liberated.

However, nothing official was announced and the internees were reluctant to leave for fear of retaliation if the rumours proved incorrect. For days Ivy and the family waited for the British troops to come and release them but nothing happened. Babsie began exploring outside the camp.

Finally, Babsie got impatient and left for home with a few others, while most of the other internees stayed on at the camp. In the days that followed there was a lot of activity as people kept coming and going, looking for loved ones. Ellen could sense a change. "When's my Daddy coming?" she would ask incessantly.

"I don't know, darling," Ivy would say, "but he will come."

Ralph and Edna spent as much time as they could together. Ivy and the children were with them when they saw Jack making his way towards them. They were so excited to see him. He had come for them. Ivy quietly explained she didn't want to leave; she wanted to wait for Justin as she was sure he would come for his family. After hugs and goodbyes, Jack left with his parents and they headed home to Muar.

CHAPTER 17
THE BITTERSWEET END OF WAR

Miles away across the South China Sea in Cambodia, close to the Vietnamese border, Justin strongly suspected the war was ending from the actions of the Japanese. They were distracted; nervous. He could tell something was happening, though he did not know that atomic bombs had decimated Hiroshima and Nagasaki. In fact, the Japanese High Command surrendered on the 15th of August 1945.

    Justin was released very soon after the Surrender. When the POWs were reunited with the British Army, Justin was given the option to be sent immediately, anywhere in the British Empire such as England or

Australia. However, this meant he would have to leave Ivy and the family behind and so he declined the offer.

Justin was also told he would soon receive an invitation to go to London. Now that the war had ended, all the POWs were going to receive a big welcome and be decorated with military honours for their contribution to the war effort. Justin was popular with his mates, many of who were going, and they were sorry when he said he would not go. He could not contemplate leaving his family again. To him, family came first.

Once discharged from the army, Justin went immediately back to Singapore to look for his family. Jack had told him that was where Ivy and the children would be. He went directly to Ivy's Aunt Inez's house where he expected to find them. He was given the unpleasant news that his family's freedom had been abruptly curtailed and they had been re-interned. He then made his way to Changi Prison, only to be told they had been moved. He could get no further information and in desperation went to all his relatives' homes looking for them. He was relieved to find his mother, Josephine, safe at his Uncle Charles' home and to know that his uncle's family had survived the ordeal.

His mother and uncle could see that Justin was exhausted and weakened by the years of near starvation and hard physical labour. They persuaded him to rest and stay the night. Justin took their advice, aware he was struggling to keep going. He was also urged to bring the family back to their home when he found them.

Justin slept for a few hours and when he awoke, he joined his mother and uncle for the evening meal. Justin's thoughts turned to his siblings and their families. His mother and uncle had waited for the right time to tell Justin what happened to family members during the war. Justin learned that his sister Patricia, had lost her husband Bertie, but she and her two boys were safe. His nephew, Quenton, the eldest son of Henrietta and Joe, was taken away by the Japanese soldiers and was never seen again. Their other children were left alone.

Then Charles disclosed what had happened to Justin's brother, Roy, when he had to leave Taman Mount Austin to present himself for registration at the Johore Civil Service Club. Roy did not return. Justin struggled with the realisation that he would never see Roy again. Charles tried to ease Justin's pain by giving him the news of the miraculous escape of Roy's wife Belle and daughter, Angela.

After a while, Charles gently said there was more to tell. Justin braced himself for further distressing news. He was to hear the fate of his eldest brother, Swithin, his wife Eileen and their beautiful, gifted daughter, Tessie.

On the 29th of April 1942, there was a big celebration in Ibu Kluang, as it was the Japanese Emperor's birthday. Tessie, their only child, who was an accomplished pianist at the age of twelve, was asked to play the piano for the occasion. One of the officers present was so taken by her, he wanted Tessie for himself. Her parents refused.

Shortly after the concert, unbeknown to Swithin and his wife, a British flag was planted on their property. In the early hours of the morning, their house was raided, the flag was found and they were accused of being pro-British. It was an act of revenge. Neighbours watched as Swithin, Eileen and daughter Tessie, were taken to the Kluang Military Airfield by the Japanese. They were executed and their bodies were buried in two graves. Justin was devastated. Tears were shed. Together, Josephine, Justin and Charles grieved for cherished family members whose lives were taken in such a cruel and violent way.

Justin knew he had to be positive. The next day, he resumed his search for his wife and children. This time he joined up with other army personnel who were also looking for loved ones. He was informed that the group were on their way to what was previously the Headquarters of the British Army and Royal Air Force in Singapore. When they reached their destination, they were taken aback to see what was once spacious and beautiful grounds turned into a huge Detention Centre: 'Sime Road Internment Camp'. As they made their way through the different sections, each of them silently hoped or prayed to see a familiar face.

Ivy, who had been on a constant lookout for her husband, saw Justin first, but was not sure it was him; he was so thin. They had last seen each other three and a half years ago, on that chaotic day in February 1942, as Singapore was about to fall. It seemed like a lifetime away. Yet, there was something familiar about him.

"Justin," she called out tentatively, and he turned!

It was a heart-rending reunion. Holding him tightly by the hand, she ushered him to the children. 'Darlings, this is your Daddy."

She had kept their father so real for them during all those years, they did not need any further introduction. They clamoured all over him. One climbed on top of his shoulders, the other sat on his knee. There was a feeling of comfort and contentment as if they had found something precious that was lost. After all these years, the father they had heard so much of, was with them at last.

Ivy and the girls were given a warm welcome and made to feel at home when they arrived at Justin's uncle's house. For Justin and Ivy, being together again as a family was a dream come true. Uncle Charles and his family graciously gave Ivy and Justin space for themselves so they could reconnect and to allow the children time to know their father better. Prayers of thanks were said that night. Both Justin and Ivy felt very humble and grateful that their little family had been spared when so many others experienced loss. The next day, after fond farewells, Justin took leave of his uncle and his mother and he and his family boarded the train for their hometown, Muar, in Malaya.

It was pitch black and Ellen remembers the sparks that flew past the window as the old steam train chugged slowly home.

EPILOGUE

The Eurasian Community

It took a while for the survivors of the Eurasian community in Muar to recover from the shock and horror of losing so many of their loved ones and friends. Morale was very low. Every family was affected in some way.

Both Justin and Ivy became involved in community work. Justin was Scout Master for many years and Ivy became Brown Owl for the Brownies.

Ivy's cousin, Enid and her husband Horace, generously opened their house for monthly meetings and social activities. They had two children, Ursula and Dawn. Eleanor (Ellen) and Jeanne (Jean) still remember the

Christmas parties and 'sing-a-longs' at the McLeod's home.

Ralph and Edna

My grandfather, Ralph, was incarcerated in Changi Prison because he was British. He bravely endured his fate, hoping his wife Edna, Ivy, and the children were safe. He was a tower of strength for Ivy and her family when they returned from the war, providing them with shelter, food and love. Bill's loss at an early age was heart-breaking for Ralph as he would never get the chance to know his son better. His grandchildren brought him joy and a special bond developed between Jean and her grandfather. To Jean and I, our grandparent's house was wonderful. It was a grand home raised on white stone pillars and flanked on either side by a white stone staircase. Ralph resumed his position as Chief Health Inspector of Muar after a period of recuperation.

Granny Edna was a shining example of faith and trust in a loving God. Though she was hard of hearing and delicate in health, she was an immeasurable help to my mother in caring for Jean and myself during the war. On her return home, her health picked up and she continued to help Mum look after us girls. I was especially close to her. My cherished memories of my grandmother are of her innumerable songs and wise sayings, her kindness, and her final words to me before I left for Australia: "Granny loves you, Ellen."

When Ralph retired, he bought a house and named it 'Flower Cottage'. He spent many hours in the garden so it would live up to its name. Edna was a gracious hostess and a very generous person. She would earn money using her catering skills, then give away not only her earnings but most of the money received as gifts from her family, to those in need. Family members loved her dearly but were exasperated at times.

After Ralph's death in 1950, Edna sold Flower Cottage and lived with Ivy and Justin for several years. She would then stay intermittently with me and my family. Edna spent her final years in Jack and Millie's home.

Jack and Millie

Uncle Jack risked his life, not only by visiting his brother Bill and Justin at their Burma-Siam Camps but also by carrying Bill and Justin's letters with him until he was finally sent back to Singapore. Had he been caught with them, it would have resulted in certain death. But he brought those letters to his mother and sister safely; such was his love for his family.

Jack was posted to Johore Bahru as Senior Health Inspector and Millie was a teacher at the local government school. They had three children, Pamela, Norma, and Ralph. Some years later they had a new addition to their family when they adopted Marianne.

Jean and I spent wonderful holidays in Johore Bahru with our cousins.

In 1957 Jack and Millie moved to Muar when Jack was appointed Chief Health Inspector, walking in his father's shoes and Millie became headmistress of the Government Girl's School.

As he grew older, Jack developed heart problems. Whenever anyone inquired about his health he would say in a spritely voice, "I'm fine". One morning, after enjoying breakfast and coffee at a café, Jack, three months short of his seventieth birthday, had a fatal heart attack.

Bill

My uncle Billy, the younger uncle, was only nineteen when captured. From all accounts, he was a caring and compassionate man. He worked untiringly as a medic, always putting the welfare of his charges before himself. He forced himself to keep going until he was at 'Death's door' itself.

Ivy and Justin

My father Justin came home a different man and always looked for calm and sanity. With the love and support of his loved ones, his hope became a reality. He picked up the threads of his life, made a stable home for his family and became a man to be admired for his wisdom, strength, and integrity.

His love and commitment to his wife and children never wavered. While at the Burma-Siam Railway camp, he endured hardship and misery but he never gave in. "I willed myself to live for my family," he simply stated.

Ivy, my mother, faced adversity early in her life and was hospitalised for much of her childhood and teen years because of a diseased hip. When the war forced on her the responsibility of caring and protecting her children, she bravely and resolutely took on the task. Ivy emerged from the war much more assertive, self-reliant and most of all, grateful, not only to her mother who was her confidante and moral support, but also to some of the Japanese captors, from whom she received kindness. "I realised that respect was important to the Japanese, so I kept to myself and always showed respect."

Mum lived up to the value, 'Do unto others as you would have others do unto you.'

For Justin and Ivy, starting life again as a family, was something they both yearned for throughout their time of separation. However, both Ivy and Justin had changed dramatically and it was hard for the couple to adjust to living with each other. Justin had become a lot quieter and somewhat introverted. The treatment he and his fellow POWs' endured on the 'Death Railway' left them all, in some way physically, mentally, and emotionally scarred. Justin remained soft spoken and gentle in his manner but was fighting his own demons. Ivy, on the other hand, had become very independent; nothing seemed too difficult to overcome. Only their deep love for each other sustained them through this challenging period.

Justin was offered a teaching position by Mrs Milne at the Government Primary English School and completed a two-year training course. He excelled as a teacher and five years later was appointed Headmaster of a primary school in the next town. A few years later he became a Lecturer at the Teachers' Day Training College in Johore Bahru.

Members of the British Civil Club approached Ivy to teach their pre-school children. They had heard she had experience in teaching young children and offered to set up a classroom in one of their homes. News of Ivy's exceptional teaching skill spread and in 1954 she established the first Kindergarten in Muar with Justin's sister, Patricia as her assistant. At age thirty-two, Ivy decided to sit for her School Leaving Certificate examination and was eventually successful. She then went on to fully qualify as a school teacher.

As parents, they could not do enough for their children. Both ensured that the children learned that 'respect' was of great importance. Sadly, Ivy and Justin lost the son they had longed for. Aloysius, delivered by Caesarean Section on 19th of May 1946 only lived for a few short hours. Ivy was told she would not be able to bear any more children.

Ivy went to Melbourne in 1966 to be with Jeanne for the birth of her son, David. Justin joined her a year later. Both gained permanent residence in Australia and resumed their teaching careers until they retired.

Justin and Ivy lived long lives and passed away peacefully, Justin in 1995 at the age of eighty-three and Ivy in 2012. She was ninety-three.

As for my sister Jeanne and I, we came through the war safe and alive but not unscathed. I was timid and nervous, and Jeanne suffered from nightmares. Yet, I was always optimistic. Mum said, "You lived in fantasyland, Eleanor. As a child, you were always singing; you would go into a world of your own". At the same time, the experience taught me resilience and courage - qualities that have held me in good stead throughout my life. I learnt to see good in people, even though I am sometimes considered as being naïve. Most of all, my faith was nurtured and strengthened by my beloved mother and grandmother.

Jean became resourceful. Though kind and generous she would not succumb to anyone's bullying despite her size and she was fiercely protective of all those close to her. She has great compassion and has a strong sense of justice, coming to the aid of anyone who needs her help.

Jeanne

In 1961, Jean was granted a Colombo Plan scholarship to do nursing in Australia. After completing her nurse's training at the Royal Melbourne Hospital, she married John (Joop) Tyssen. They have two sons, David, and Eric. While bringing up the children at home, Jean took up studying as an interest. It would lead her to swap from nursing to teaching and eventually take up the position of Mathematics Coordinator at a large government College in Melbourne, which she held until she retired at age fifty-five.

A couple of years later, Jean decided to do a refresher course at St Vincent Hospital to regain her nursing qualification. She spent the next ten years working part-time, first as a District Nurse and then at a Rehabilitation Hospital.

Though now fully retired, Jean is actively involved in community activities. She and Joop have three grandchildren.

Eleanor

In January 1958, Eleanor left Muar for Singapore where she took up nursing. She married Malcolm Nunis in 1962 and in the following years had a daughter Jean-Marie and then a son, Christopher. Sadly, their darling daughter passed away in May 1966, before the age of three. Their second son, Trevor was born in October 1967.

After working in Operating Theatre at Singapore General Hospital, Eleanor did a specialist theatre course in Melbourne, Australia and on her return to Singapore was appointed Nurse-In-Charge of the Plastic and Reconstructive Surgery Theatre.

In 1976, Eleanor, Malcolm and their boys, Christopher and Trevor migrated to Melbourne. It was a wonderful family reunion. At last Justin's wish for his family to settle in Australia was realised. There was jubilation in December of the same year when a third son, Mark, was born to Eleanor and Malcolm. Justin and Ivy were now the proud grandparents of five grandsons.

Eleanor continued with her nursing career and became Theatre Supervisor of the Operating Suite at a Private Hospital in Melbourne.

She and Malcolm are now retired. It was a time of great sadness when Alexander, their youngest grandson passed away in October 2012. They feel blessed that they presently have eight grandchildren who bring them great joy, and two great-grandsons.

REFLECTION

War seems to unearth the deepest roots of evil in the hearts of human beings. The lust for power and control can cause man to become bitter with hatred, greed, and revenge. Persecutions, atrocities, and wanton disregard for human rights result. The world is plunged into mayhem and the unfortunate innocent pay the price.

But from the depths of confusion, despair and chaos, Goodness, inherent in mankind, peeps through. It defies evil fleetingly, offering a glimpse of hope and succour, reflecting the Goodness of God.

Every good and perfect gift
comes from above.

– James 1:17

FAMILY TREE

Robert Miles
m. Agnes Le Fevre

James Stanley
m. Sarah ...

Thomas Miles
m. Eleanor Phipps

Frederick Stanley
m. Elizabeth Harding

Edna Miles married Ralph Stanley

Siblings
Stanley, John
Muriel, Inez
Sybil, Daryl
Cuthbert, Brenda
Mavis

Siblings
Frank
Ethel
Arthur

Ivy Stanley
m. Justin Monteiro

William Stanley
(Bill)

Norman Stanley
(Jack)
m. Millicent Rodrigues
(Millie)

Eleanor   Jeanne   Pamela Norma Ralph Marianne

Jack and Millie Stanley were married on 3rd of June 1944.

Eleanor's 7th birthday at Muar in 1947 with Jeanne.

Eleanor, Ivy, Justin, and Jeanne c. 1957 Muar.

*Justin's youngest brother Oswald (Osie) Monteiro
with his OBE medal for services to the local
community, c.1960. He was principal of the
Blind School in Johore Bahru.*

Eleanor and Malcolm Nunis were married on the 20th of October 1962, in Singapore.

Jeanne and John (Joop) Tyssen were married on the 30th of January, 1965 in Melbourne Australia.

Ivy and Babsie were reunited after 50 years.

Ivy (left) recounted her story on being interred in Changi Prison for a feature in New Idea magazine in 1995, marking the 50th anniversary of the end of the Pacific War.

Jean and Eleanor endured three years in Changi with their mum Ivy.

Ivy Monteiro's 93rd Birthday, Melbourne Australia 2012.

(Front row from left): Sean, Bridget, Montana, Tyeisha, Kaija, Zach & Nathan. (Middle row from left): Malcolm, Ivy, Sue, Jadon & Chris. (Standing 3rd row from left): John, Marianne, Angela, Delise, Eleanor, Jeanne, Denise & Robert. (Standing back row from left): Eric, David, Mark, John (Joop).

Tyssen Family, Melbourne, Australia, 2008. Clockwise: John, Lynne, Eric, David, Liam, Jeanne and Bridget.
(Not in picture – Tracey and Sean)

Trevor Nunis and family Melbourne, Australia 2010.
Clockwise: Deborah, Peter, Trevor, Alexander and Nathan.

AUTHOR'S NOTE

This story is my personal tribute to my mother and father, Ivy and Justin, grandparents, Ralph and Edna, and uncles, Jack and Bill.

The sufferings they went through during the Second World War were sometimes unimaginable but their courage, sacrifices and their concern, not so much for themselves but for their family and for the people who shared in their lives during that time, was admirable.

My main purpose is to keep alive the memories and stories of this incredible group of people for current and future generations.

ACKNOWLEDGEMENTS & SOURCES

Unsung Heroes has evolved from two short stories of my parents' experiences during the war and I sincerely thank the following people for their contributions:

Joan Ryan, a retired English teacher and volunteer with Palliative Care, who was my mother, Ivy's, biographer. Later she assisted me in editing my stories. When I decided to convert it into a book, she was invaluable in offering ideas and support. Her counsel and guidance throughout the process are deeply appreciated.

David Miller, the publisher of DM Books in Singapore had advertised for short stories about World War II to be compiled into a book. I sent him the two stories and he suggested I combine and expand them into a book of my own. He has generously given advice and assistance in the process of publishing *Unsung Heroes*.

Words cannot express my gratitude to **Jeanne**, my younger sister, who has been my editor these last eighteen months. She has painstakingly worked on the book, researching, contributing, spending countless hours shaping the book to what it is now. Her love and support have been incredible. Special thanks to **Joop**, Jeanne's husband, whose encouragement, support and patience enabled Jean to spend the long hours working with me.

To **David Tyssen**, my nephew, my heartfelt thanks. He has enthusiastically and tirelessly researched and verified events described in the story. He has also contacted people and various organisations involved in World War II. Besides proof-reading, David has made valuable recommendations for consideration. He took on the task of photo-editing, sorting the numerous images included in the book and is responsible for the beautiful cover design.

Grateful thanks to **Eric Tyssen**, my nephew, for his loving support, suggestions, and proofreading. I would like to express my gratitude to David and Eric's wives, **Tracey and Lynne** for their generous support.

I would like to thank the curators of and contributors to the **Muntok Peace Museum** website which serves to honour and remember the Palembang and Muntok Internees of World War II. In particular, **Dr**

Judy Balcombe for her interest in my story. Her connections with a vast network of people whose loved ones were caught up in the Fall of Singapore, has been so helpful. Through her, my family has opened up previously unknown avenues of inquiry, including **Vilma Howe** (nee Stubbs) and **Jonathan Moffatt**.

Vilma and her family also tried to escape from Singapore on board the *S.S. Mata Hari* as my family did in 1942. Although a young girl at the time, her fond memories of Edna and Ivy in the camps in Sumatra really inspired me during the writing of the story.

Jonathan Moffatt from the Malayan Volunteers Group (MVG) has provided fantastic support and information on various members of the family through the process. And I would like to thank **Jane Nielsen** from MVG for providing the Civilian and POW camps in Sumatra map for me to use in the book.

I want to thank **Adam Johnson** for his help and technical know-how on the use of Adobe Photoshop and his work on the front cover of this book.

Thanks to the **Australian Eurasian Association of WA Inc** for some of the details on events related to my story.

For the inclusion of many of the war-related photos in my book, I would like to thank the **Australian War Memorial** and the people who contributed such a rich and vast array of photos to the collection.

I would like to express my gratitude to the many relatives and friends who gave useful comments, loving support and encouragement especially: My cousins **Pavril (Pavy)** and **Jean Monteiro**, who have most generously contacted our relatives who could contribute photos to the story; my cousin **David Monteiro** who has given of his time to photograph scenes of Muar, especially of the Tanjung and the Mosque featured in the story; **Christopher Chase-Currier** who gave valuable information on some of the family members involved in the story; the **Open Door Team, Joanne Morrison** and members of my writing group for their encouragement and suggestions and in particular, Joanne Morrison for her assistance.

Finally, my beloved sons, **Christopher**, **Trevor** and **Mark** and their families who have supported me throughout this journey with love and encouragement, always ready with advice and practical assistance, especially with the computer, forms to fill or any tasks I was unable to handle.

Last, but not least, to my dear husband, **Malcolm**, for his love, understanding and patience, most of all, for a listening ear. Your encouragement and support have enabled me to achieve my dream of writing this book.

ANOTHER BOOK BY ELEANOR NUNIS

A collection of uplifting verses and music to reflect a journey walked in the presence of God

Another publication by

www.ingramcontent.com/pod-product-compliance
Lightning Source LLC
Chambersburg PA
CBHW060828050426
42453CB00008B/622